The Political Economy of Taxation

The Political Economy of Taxation

Lessons from Developing Countries

Paola Profeta

Bocconi University, Italy

Simona Scabrosetti

University of Pavia, Italy

Edward Elgar

Cheltenham, UK • Northampton, MA, USA

Published by
Edward Elgar Publishing Limited
The Lypiatts
15 Lansdown Road
Cheltenham
Glos GL50 2JA
UK

Edward Elgar Publishing, Inc.
William Pratt House
9 Dewey Court
Northampton
Massachusetts 01060
USA

A catalogue record for this book
is available from the British Library

Library of Congress Control Number: 2009938389

Mixed Sources
Product group from well-managed
forests and other controlled sources
www.fsc.org Cert no. SA-COC-1565
© 1996 Forest Stewardship Council
FSC

ISBN 978 1 84844 071 5

Printed and bound by MPG Books Group, UK

Contents

Figures

Tables

Preface

The initial idea to develop this project was born when we were working together on a series of contributions focused on political economy issues of taxation in different areas of the world. Our task was to describe the main political factors which played a major role in the design of the tax system and in the implementation of tax reforms in some specific countries. These works increased our interest towards developing countries, in particular those which have recently experienced an economic transition toward a market economy and/or a political transition toward democratic institutions. We found that in these countries the foundation of democracy and its consolidation over time, as opposed to the presence of autocratic regimes, as well as other political elements, such as the role of lobbies or interest groups, are important factors in the analysis of tax level and tax design. They may interact with the main macroeconomic variables, such as the level of GDP per worker, the openness of the economy, the level of debt and the share of agriculture, and with other socio-economic factors, such as the age of the population, female labour force participation, urbanization, population density, schooling enrolment and the extension of the shadow economy.

Many rigorous empirical studies have analysed developing countries and their political regimes with the objective of explaining their development and growth. The analysis of tax systems and in particular the tax composition of these countries has instead received much more limited attention from the applied political economy literature. We thus decided to start this project as an attempt to develop a detailed and comprehensive empirical analysis. Such a quantitative approach implies a collection of political, fiscal, macroeconomic and socio-demographic data for a large set of countries and for a certain time span. We decided to narrow our attention to two critical world areas, Asia and Latin America, and collect data for as many countries as possible in these two areas. We also decided that it would be useful to collect data for new EU member countries and use them for comparisons. Finally, owing mainly to the availability of comparable data, we restricted our attention to the time period starting in the 1990s. We had this idea in the back of our minds when we met Matthew Pitman, who encouraged us to submit our project to the Editorial Office of Edward Elgar Publishers.

The collection of data has not been an easy task, especially for those countries where the official international statistics do not provide organized or online information. We are grateful to several people who helped us during this process, in particular Maria Victoria Espada from CEPAL and Roberta Gatti from the World Bank.

We gratefully acknowledge Luigi Bernardi and Vito Tanzi for encouraging us to develop this big project and for their useful comments. We also benefited from discussions and contacts with many researchers at several stages of this project: Alberto Barreix, Matteo Cacciatore, Angela Fraschini, Vincenzo Galasso, Luca Gandullia, Anna Marenzi, Riccardo Puglisi, Parthasarathi Shome and Stanley Winer.

Some of the ideas developed in the book were presented in preliminary forms at national and international conferences, in particular at the annual meetings of the Italian Society of Public Economics and the annual meetings of the International Institute of Public Finance of recent years, as well as seminars at the University of Pavia, OECD, Stockholm University and the University of Tallinn.

Financial support from the Italian Ministry of University and the University of Pavia is gratefully acknowledged.

We are indebted to our editor, Matthew Pitman, for his great incentives and support.

Special thanks go to Paola Salardi for excellent research assistance with the manuscript, tables and figures.

Although we are grateful for all the help received, we are responsible for any errors that may have remained in the book.

1. Introduction

Taxation is a major issue in economics and politics. Tax design and the implementation of tax reforms are at the core of economic policy. They are also among the more debated issues in the political arena. In modern democracies tax reforms need the support of voters in order to be implemented, while at the same time policy makers try to design a tax system and propose tax reforms to attract and please as many voters as possible. The issue of taxation can attract and alter votes, in particular those of uncertain citizens (who may be a large part of the electorate) who decide which party to vote for by computing the advantages, even (and, in some cases, mainly) fiscal ones, that they could enjoy from this party as opposed to the opponents (Hettich and Winer, 1999; Profeta, 2007).

In traditionally non-democratic countries the process underlying tax decisions is much more difficult and less clear to predict. Lobby groups and interest groups that are economically and politically powerful have a dominant role. And when these countries experience a democratic transition it is very likely that these influences will remain strong and interact with voters' preferences in determining tax policy outcomes.

Democratic and economic transitions are generally strictly related (Boix, 2003). In many areas of the world the economic transition goes hand-in-hand with a political transition towards a modern concept and organization of democracy. Although it is difficult to establish the correct direction of a causal relationship, there may be positive feedback effects between economic and political reforms (Giavazzi and Tabellini, 2005).

The interplay between economic and political factors may prove crucial to understanding public policies and reforms. Taxation is a central issue. The transition towards a free market crucially affects the economic status of a country and the push towards a modern design of tax system through the implementation of several reforms. Thus, both economic and political transformations have an impact

on the fiscal decisions, the design of tax systems and the implementation of tax reforms in developing countries.

Taxes (and public spending) are expected to increase under a democratic regime, to satisfy the needs of the electorate. However, the
empirical evidence is not uncontroversial. Moreover, what should
happen to the structure of taxation is much less clear and typically
neglected by the existing empirical analysis.

This book develops a unified applied political economy analysis
of taxation with reference to two key areas of developing countries:
Asia and Latin America. We also look at new EU member states
in a comparative perspective for the time period between 1995 and
2004. We are constrained to this time interval since 1995 is the first
available year for homogeneous fiscal data of the new EU member
countries and 2004 is the last available year for fiscal data of Asian
countries.[1] These countries share some common trends in their transitions towards a free market and/or a modern democracy. However,
the history and pattern of development in these areas show different
features and timing: in Latin American countries the democratic
transition is a quite recent event, while Asian countries show a recent
fast economic transition, but are still in trouble with the democratic
one. This justifies our approach, which will first analyse each area
separately. Then we make a comparison with new EU member countries, which have almost completed their transition both in economics and in politics.

We develop an integrating framework to study the economic and
political issues related to taxation in these economies. To do this,
we build a unified dataset including political, fiscal, macroeconomic
and socio-demographic data for a large set of countries of each area.
Data are collected from different comparable sources (see Chapter 7
for the details) and are used in a set of cross-country regressions. We
pay particular attention to the political variables, that is measures of
democracy, which are collected by the most used datasets available,
Polity IV and Freedom House. Using different indicators does not
change our results, which is a robustness check of our findings.

Our analysis shows that fiscal pressure is still very low in transition countries with respect to developed ones. We argue however
that it is reasonable to expect that this fiscal pressure will rise, for
instance in Asia, under social transformations and the related rising
demand for government to assume more responsibility towards the
unemployed, poor, sick and elderly. We find that more democratic

countries generally show a higher level of tax revenue, even when a certain number of control variables are included and robustness checks are performed. The results on the structure of taxation are much less clear, and more democratic countries are not necessarily associated with more personal income taxes, which are typically more redistributive, than autocratic ones. This happens for instance in the Latin American area, where we argue that this result depends on the role played by vested interests and the financial sector.

The book is organized as follows. After this brief introduction, Chapter 2 reviews the main findings of the theoretical and empirical political economy literature on democracies. We first analyse the socio-economic conditions that could favour the foundation and the consolidation of a democratic system and then focus on the two-way relation between democracy and growth. Finally, we study the impact of democracy on redistributive policies, mainly taxation.

Chapter 3 provides an overview of the main economic (GDP per worker, share of agriculture on GDP, sum of exports and imports on GDP, central government debt on GDP, Gini index), socio-demographic (the secondary school enrolment, the share of over 65s in the population, the female labour force participation rate, urbanization, population density, the size of the shadow economy on GDP) and political (different measures of democracy) variables which may play a role in explaining the level of tax revenue. We look at data of the complete sample of Asian, Latin American and new EU member countries and we provide correlations, which are plotted in graphs. We then look at the relation between our measures of democracy and the level of specific taxes.

Chapters 4 and 5 are devoted to our two critical areas of analysis: Asia and Latin America. For a selected sample of countries in each area we perform cross-country regressions to understand the determinants of the level of taxation and of the structure of taxation. Our attention is focused on the role played by political variables, in particular the level of democracy, which turns out to be positively and significantly associated with the level of tax revenue. The relation with the structure of taxation however, mainly direct versus indirect taxes, and the level of social security contributions, is not unambiguous.

Finally, Chapter 6 develops a comparison between Asian, Latin American and new EU member countries and provides some conclusions.

NOTE

1. Our source of fiscal data for new EU members is Eurostat. From 1995, national accounts data are generally available in the ESA95 (European System of Accounts 95) format.

2. The political economy of democracies: a review of the literature

The existing political economy literature on democracies deals with two important questions: (i) what are the socio-economic determinants of democracy, if any? (ii) does democracy affect public policies, mainly in terms of growth and redistribution?

In this chapter we provide a short review of the current theoretical and empirical findings on these issues within the political economy literature. In the first section we focus on the socio-economic conditions that could favour the foundation and consolidation of a democratic system,[1] following the analysis of the structural approach as well as the strategic approach to the political change. Then, in the second section we consider the two-way relation between democracy and growth. Finally, in the third section we deal with the impact of democracy on redistributive public policies with a specific focus on taxation.

2.1 DEMOCRACY AND ITS DETERMINANTS

Following Acemoglu and Robinson's (2006) theory, democracy is a situation of political equality,[2] implying a transfer of the *de jure* political power from the elites (the rich) to the citizens (the poor). Starting from a non-democracy, in which the elites have *de jure* political power, a revolutionary threat by the citizens, who have the *de facto* political power[3], could lead to repression, which will be really attractive only in particular cases, mainly if it is neither too risky nor too costly for the elites.[4] In all other cases, the threat will wring promises by the elites to future pro-citizen policies. To make these concessions credible, a formal transfer of the *de jure* political power from the elites to the majority of citizens is needed, meaning that democratization has to happen. In this way, the majority of the population will be allowed to vote and express their preferences about policies and the government will represent the preferences of the whole population. In other words, being a regime more beneficial to the majority, democracy will result in policies relatively more favourable to it (i.e. redistribution)[5].

Obviously, democratization is a complex historical process. It starts with the decline of an authoritarian regime and the beginning of a new representative political system which, through its consolidation, reaches its full maturity (Shin, 1994). The transition stage is characterized by great political instability, which generally ends with the promulgation of a new constitution and free and fair elections, that is when elite consensus on procedures goes hand-in-hand with extensive mass participation in elections and other institutional processes (Higley and Gunther, 1992). This consolidation stage usually takes decades to complete its course. It could also be hindered by the nature of political institutions, which may allow the elites to influence democracy's choices to avoid radical majoritarian (populist) policies (this is what happens in a formal democracy). In other words, although there exist democratic institutions, actual policies may be constrained by anti-democratic provisions in the new constitution, and the voices of some people may be louder thanks to lobbying, bribery and other types of persuasion which aim at protecting the interests of the most powerful groups in the society (O'Donnell, 1988). As a consequence, the vertical conflict between politicians and their constituencies should be considered, not only because of the risk of corruption, but also because policy makers may be self-interested and may want to pursue their own agenda. However, given the credible threat of losing power in the next election, in a democratic system political accountability will generally be high (Boix, 2003).

Can the transition process to democracy and its subsequent consolidation be favoured by particular socio-economic circumstances?

Certainly, economic crises and macroeconomic shocks determine fluctuations in *de facto* political power. By raising discontent and undermining the legitimacy and survival of the authoritarian regime, they can effectively help to promote democracy (Haggard and Kaufman, 1995).

Moreover, following 'modernization theory' (Lipset, 1959), economic development, and in particular the rise of the level of per capita income, would induce citizens to no longer tolerate repressive regimes.[6] Countries should become more democratic as they become more modern and more complex, urbanization rises, the importance of industry increases, agriculture commercializes and is no longer characterized by feudal or semi-feudal labour relations, the *bourgeoisie* becomes strong and education attainment improves. Developed economies and political democracies should consequently emerge and survive together, especially in the long run. Markets would thus prosper in a political framework characterized by constitutional liberties and democratic practices. In fact, income growth and industrialization lead to a wealthy, well-organized and pluralistic society in which the mass of the population can intelligently participate in politics and avoid succumbing to irresponsible demagogues, repression becomes more difficult, power is widely distributed and the cost of toleration of the opposition by the incumbent in the policy-making process becomes low (Dahl, 1971).[7] In such a context, democratization can more easily occur.

In addition, the process of economic modernization generally results in both enlarging the middle class, who act as a moderating political force, a buffer between the opposite interests of the elites and the citizens, and reducing income inequality, which is a source of political conflict that may even lead to authoritarian solutions. As the distribution of income becomes more equal among individuals, redistributive pressures from the poor on the rich diminish and the probability of a peaceful transition from an authoritarian regime to universal suffrage increases. The ultimate level of taxes becomes smaller than the cost of repression. On the contrary, when the redistributive demands of the worse-off citizens on the rich are particularly intense, the latter will strongly oppose the introduction of democracy, which would allow heavy taxes to be levied on them. Thus, inter-group inequality should be at an intermediate level to make redistribution suitable and avoid repressive non-democracies or revolutions. In this sense, the opposition of the rich to universal suffrage would also reduce with the credible commitment of the poor to moderate levels of redistribution according to the fact that low taxes stimulate faster economic growth (Boix, 2003).

Moreover, social mobility across classes would foster democracy by easing social conflict, that is by tending to equalize the income of individuals over time.[8] The nature of the assets owned by the elites would also matter, given that for example land is easier to tax and less damaged by social and political turmoil than physical and human capital.

Modernization also means both the raising of education levels and the creation of a labour force required to make its own decisions in the production process (an autonomous labour force). The crucial idea is that education promotes democracy either because it enables a culture of democracy to develop or because it leads to greater prosperity. As a consequence, the toleration of different values and options and the recourse to liberal democracy as the mechanism to settle disagreements should increase. On the other side, capitalist development reduces the power of the elites (landlord class) and raises the political importance and the organizational ability of the working and middle classes (Therborn, 1977; Rueschemeyer *et al.*, 1992).

The role of capital mobility in favouring democratization is also crucial. Democracy would prevail when not only economic equality but also capital mobility is high in a given country. A reduction in the cost of moving capital away implies that government must curb taxes. As a consequence, the extent of political conflict among capital holders and non-holders declines and the probability of democracy rises. On the contrary, when they cannot escape the threat of high taxes shifting assets abroad, capital owners want to block democracy. In this sense, the association between economic development and democracy comes from the transformation that capital experiences with economic modernization: from an economy based on fixed assets to an economy based on highly mobile capital, in which the accumulation of human capital, harder to expropriate than the physical one, increases (Boix, 2003).

At the same time, the early non-democratic regime would be important in order to determine the type of democracy that emerges after its collapse. Starting from a totalitarian or a sultanistic regime, for example, would imply the solving of different kinds of problems when democracy takes place (Linz and Stepan, 1996).

In addition to these domestic factors, international factors would also play a relevant role in the democratization process. In this sense, globalization would favour the transition to representative political systems. In particular, financial integration would make it more difficult to tax the elites; increased international trade would reduce the inequality between the rich and the poor by increasing the rewards to labour and reducing those to capital;[9] and increased political integration would make repression easier to sanction (Acemoglu and Robinson, 2006). Moreover, the pressures to democratization from neighbouring or other countries[10] and from international organizations have to be considered. However, the best thing the international agencies would have to do to promote democracy is establish particular conditions to make the transition and the consolidation process easier without attempting to impose any foreign practice or rule. Finally, the mass media, acting as information providers, could also make people less willing to tolerate authoritarian regimes (Shin, 1994).

Many empirical analyses have been devoted to explicitly testing the different theoretical predictions about the socio-economic determinants of democracy and its consolidation. Boix (2003) finds a positive relation between the level of per capita income and the stability of the democratic system, even if the level of per capita income simply appears as a proxy for other more important variables such as the average years of education, the level of economic concentration, the share of agriculture over GDP and the size of the oil sector.[11] However, both the level of inequality and asset specificity seem to be the main factors related to the introduction and consolidation of a democratic political system. In short, highly unequal countries remain authoritarian and, whenever they go through a democratic phase, it is only a temporary phase. At the same time, countries with a limited share of mobile assets are unlikely to become democratic unless they show a particularly equal income distribution.

Epstein *et al.* (2005)[12] empirically find support for the modernization hypothesis: a higher per capita income not only increases the likelihood of a movement away from autocracy, but also decreases the likelihood of a movement away from democracy. They also underline the importance of looking at partial or unconsolidated democracies whose behaviour would affect the level, rate and properties of the democratic transition.

According to Barro (1996, 1999), GDP per worker, the level of primary schooling, the absence of gender discrimination in education opportunities, country size measured in terms of population, life expectancy at birth, low income inequality, the size of the middle class, and to a lower extent reduced ethnic fragmentation, non-colony status[13] and Protestant religious belief are positively related to democracy. As a consequence, democracy would catch on after reasonable standards of living have been attained, whereas would seem not to last without strong economic bases.

This result is in line with Glaeser *et al.* (2004). Their empirical evidence shows that constraints on the executive do not lead to growth, while human capital does. Only after accumulating human and physical capital and becoming richer are countries more likely to democratize.[14]

Moreover, economic crises, defined as a sudden and significant reduction in the growth rate, increase the probability of democratization. In particular it seems that economic shocks do not affect transitions away from democracy, but rather they lead to the collapse of dictatorships (Acemoglu *et al.*, 2005).

Finally, do political institutions matter for democracy stability and consolidation? At least from a theoretical point of view, proportional rather than majoritarian representation, parliamentary rather than presidential system and federal rather than central government structure representation should ensure more democratic stability. In fact, in proportional regimes, the median voter does not vary election to election; in parliamentary systems, minorities are not excluded from the decision process and both the political tension and the political conflict among opposite candidates are less deep; and finally decentralization reduces the redistributive contrast between richer and poorer areas. However, according to Boix (2003), these differences in terms of political institutions and democracy stability are not so relevant. Contrary to the predictions of the institutionalist literature, his empirical analysis shows that only federalism may reduce the probability of a democratic breakdown. In short, weak institutions, such as electoral rules, may not affect the chances of democratic survival, while strong institutions, such as a politically decentralized government structure, can do it by altering the balance of power among contending parties.[15]

Summing up, a higher level of economic well-being, which entails higher rates of literacy, education and urbanization, and also a larger middle class, and some other structural conditions would be necessary, though not sufficient, for democracy to be widely supported and then introduced. As underlined by many political scientists,[16] the will of political leaders is essential. In other words, specific groups' strength or specific sets of interactions are necessary for the actual establishment of democratic institutions (Huntington, 1991). Democratic politics do not merely grow out of socio-economic and cultural bases, but they can be promoted, and then survive and grow even when structural and cultural factors are not favourable (Lijphart, 1990). Human will and action will ultimately determine the success of democratization (Di Palma, 1990). The structural and the actor-based approaches thus should stay side-by-side.

2.2   DEMOCRACY AND GROWTH: A TWO-WAY RELATION

In this section we enrich the previous arguments, by showing that not only would economic development promote the foundation and the consolidation of democracy, but also stable democracies would entail economic growth. Thus, a two-way interaction between modernization and democratization is in place and it is difficult to know the correct direction of causality.

According to Persson and Tabellini (2007), democracy affects economic outcomes (economic growth) through expectations about its future stability. In other words, the current economic performance will depend on the belief in a stable democratic political system. The consolidation of democracy thus becomes fundamental, that is the accumulation of domestic and foreign 'democratic capital' becomes relevant for economic growth. In a virtuous circle, economic development would help a further consolidation of a democratic system and contribute to yet more economic growth[17] (see also Hayek, 1960; Gerring *et al.*, 2005).

The merits of democracy appear in the long run, as argued also by Papaioannou and Siourounis (2008). The accumulation of democratic capital implies a higher growth level: on average the annual growth would accelerate by 0.7 to 1.1 per cent. In particular, immediately after the transition to democracy there would be an increase in the growth rate; then growth seems to fluctuate for some years and, after the consolidation of democratic institutions, it would stabilize at a higher rate than before. Moreover, democratization may affect growth through institutional improvements rather than other mechanisms such as capital accumulation or fiscal and trade policies. On the contrary, both the anticipation effect, that is that growth starts to increase even before the transition if firms and individuals foresee the collapse of the autocratic regime, and the fact that non-democratic countries can implement growth-enhancing policies to try to stay in power are not important.

An average growth acceleration of about 1 per cent which follows a transition from an autocratic to a democratic political system is also found by Persson and Tabellini (2007). At the same time, when democracy collapses, the growth rate reduces by almost 2 per cent on average, producing a fall of about 45 per cent in per capita income.

The short-run effects of democratic transition on growth are investigated by Rodrik and Wacziarg (2005). By analysing the within-country variation, they find that these effects are positive when political transition is compared to no regime change mainly in low-income countries, countries with high ethnic fragmentation and African countries.

Democracy would also indirectly improve growth through economic liberalization, even if it may lead to worse economic outcomes immediately after the beginning of political transition, mainly because of political uncertainty and short-term political goals. Furthermore, better economic performances tend to reinforce democracy but do not affect economic liberalization (Fidrmuc, 2003).

Persson (2005) underlines that the *form* of democracy has to be considered to evaluate its impact on growth-promoting policies. Parliamentary, proportional and permanent democracies tend to enhance growth through structural policies such as trade liberalization and the protection of property rights more than the presidential, majoritarian and temporary ones. Moreover, given that parliamentary democracies also raise government spending, a positive and robust effect on economic performance is more difficult to identify.

On the contrary, Huntington (1968) shows that political stability matters for growth, independently of particular political institutions. However, political instability would reduce growth exclusively in autocratic regimes (Przeworski *et al.*, 2000). This implies that political instability cannot be defined independently of political institutions because some events (i.e. alternation in office, strikes or other manifestations of opposition) constitute instability only under dictatorships, while they are inherent in democracies. As a consequence the economy will not suffer from them. Moreover the growth rate of total income will be the same under democratic and non-democratic systems, while per capita income will grow more rapidly under democracy because of a lower rate of population growth.[18]

Furthermore, countries which undertake both reforms have better economic performance as compared to countries which undertake only economic or political liberalization (Giavazzi and Tabellini, 2005). In other words, the effects are not additive and moreover the sequence may matter. Following the 'easy path', that is first becoming a democracy and then opening up the economy, leads to poorer economic pay-offs in terms of growth, investment, trade volume and macro-policies. It is less likely that an authoritarian regime will open up the economy, but when it happens it is because interest groups opposing free trade and the market system have been crushed. Consequently, liberalization is more effective and devoid of compromises. On the other hand, it could be that better democracies arise in an open economic environment. Redistributive conflicts could weaken a young democracy characterized by a closed economy, whereas openness to trade, competition and growth, which comes from economic liberalization, provides the resources for the redistribution that a democracy requires.

On the contrary, starting from the issue of reverse causality and the risk that there are some factors which simultaneously affect both democracy and economic development, Acemoglu *et al.* (2004, 2005) empirically find no positive relation between per capita income and democracy or between education and democracy and no evidence of a causal effect of income on democracy.[19] In order to explain the strong cross-sectional correlation between income and democracy, the authors thus mainly refer to historical factors, such as the colonization experience with reference to European colonies, which in the long run persistently influence either the economic or the political development path of societies.[20]

Finally, some studies have also emphasized that democracy appears harmful for economic growth. For example, Barro (1996) finds that democracy is not a key factor for economic growth. Although democratic institutions limit the possibility of public officials carrying out non-productive investments and accumulating personal wealth, there are some growth-retarding features of democracy that have to be taken into account, such as the tendency to income redistribution and the role of interest groups. The relation between democracy and growth thus appears non-linear. More democracy would lead to higher growth levels when political freedom is low. But, with a moderate degree of political freedom, democracy would slow down growth. More generally, Fernandez and Rodrik (1991) show that growth-enhancing reforms will not be supported *ex ante* by rational voters if gainers and losers are not easy to identify. Then the status quo will be maintained. But the *ex ante* hostility could also become an *ex post* support when reforms actually turn out to be quite popular. In these cases, autocracy, rather than democracy, may lead to the reform's implementation.[21]

2.3   DEMOCRACY AND REDISTRIBUTION

Democratization allows poor groups to take part in politics and, as a consequence, should be related to policies that favour such groups and tend to promote equality. Thus, following Acemoglu and Robinson (2006) and Boix (2003)'s theories, democracy would lead to redistribution from the rich (the elites) to the poor (the citizens). This redistribution can take place both through an enlarged welfare state and through a reorganized and heavier tax system in which, in particular, direct taxes would have to become more and more employed in preference to indirect ones. In fact, representative institutions can be seen as a concession from the authoritarian rulers to raise taxation, especially, when the tax base is more elastic (see also Bates and Lien, 1985; Bates, 1991; Rogowski, 1998; and Tilly, 2004).

However, following Mulligan *et al.* (2004), there are two very different perspectives on constructing positive theories of the public sector. The first one comes from the formal voting literature, whereas the second one relates to the Chicago Political Economic School. In the formal voting literature three tenets of democratic decision making would imply democratic–non-democratic policy gaps. In other words, it would be possible to predict public policy starting from a measure of democracy and holding constant economic and demographic variables. In particular, the first tenet says that in many formal models the voting process mitigates the expression of strong policy preferences, which determines inefficient policy outcomes. The second tenet concerns the distribution of political power. This would be more equal than the distribution of income or wealth and, as a consequence, democracy would massively redistribute from rich to poor, while under authoritarian regimes the level of redistributive spending should be minimal. The third tenet of the formal voting theory emphasizes the importance of 'the form of the voting game'. On the contrary, there are positive theories of public policy such as those of Barro (1979) and Wittman (1989) that focus on efficiency considerations as the main determinants of public policy. There is no room for political factors. These theories are also related to Stigler (1970), Peltzman (1980) and Becker (1983)'s works, that is to the Chicago Political Economic School.

Empirical evidences are not uncontroversial. Boix (2003) suggests that a significant share of the public sector depends on the political regime in place, which also interacts with the distribution of income, the people's preferences and the economic conditions. Welfare expenditure may rise only after the introduction of a democratic system. In particular, the author distinguishes between redistributive expenditure, public investment and insurance programmes. Under a non-democratic regime the size of the public sector should be small, a substantial part of the electorate being excluded from the decision-making process. So, independent of the type of economy, the level of redistributive spending should be minimal. A transition to democracy, on the contrary, should raise taxes and public spending in accordance with the electoral turnout and the position of the median voter, but also with the underlying economic and social structure. The electoral turnout will thus play a fundamental role, since only when the number of low-income voters who vote is significant will the level of taxes and transfers be high.[22] In representative regimes redistribution will take place also depending on the extent of economic development. Democratic institutions can take root in farmer economies characterized by little income difference among individuals. In this case, the public sector will not grow, as redistributive tensions are practically non-existent. But democracies can also develop in industrialized societies where income equality and capital mobility are moderate. By creating an urban working class and the bases for an older population which cannot any longer receive informal family help, the industrialization process will thus raise stronger pressures for intragenerational and also intergenerational transfers, that is for increasing, redistributive public spending.

On the contrary, the level of public investment should especially depend on the economic rather than political conditions. Still, the political regime could be important if one considers that in authoritarian systems the median voter is richer than in democratic systems and, as a consequence, the incentive to invest would be higher in the first than in the second regime. However these differences would disappear as income increases.

The volatility of the income will also affect the magnitude of the welfare state. If the fluctuation of income increases (for example as a consequence of industrial accidents or joblessness) and informal family help is not contemplated, then voters who are averse to risk may want to stabilize their economic position by raising public spending. The political regime will not be relevant when the distribution of income volatility is uniform. But, if the risk is concentrated among the worse-off (well-off), public insurance schemes will increase only in a democratic (autocratic) political system.

A different result is reached by Mulligan *et al.* (2004). For a sample of 142 countries in the period 1960–90, they find that none of the different measures of public spending that they consider (government consumption, education spending and social spending, that is pension and non-pension programmes, as a percentage of GDP) is statistically different in democracies and non-democracies. However, a dummy variable that captures whether a country has been communist for more than a few years suggests that totalitarian countries spend more of their GDP on education and also on pension and non-pension programmes. Though there are no significant economic or social policy differences between representative and non-representative systems, democracies are also less likely to use anti-competitive policies that might affect public office competition, erecting political entry barriers (such as torture, the death penalty, press censorship, regulation of religion and maintaining an army; see Tullock, 1987), than non-democracies. The authors also find that democracies have flatter personal income tax structures and a generally lower tax revenue/GDP than non-democracies.

These results are in contrast with the classical prediction of Musgrave (1969) that more autocratic countries, which directly control the economy and, in particular, wages, rely more on corporate rather than on individual taxes than more democratic ones.

A fairly recent work by Kenny and Winer (2006) is explicitly devoted to the analysis of the structure of taxation in a large sample of democratic and non-democratic countries. They find that more rights and liberties, that is more democracy, lead to a more intensive use of personal income taxation. According to the authors this happens because personal income taxes are more complicated and rely on voluntary compliance,[23] rather than for redistributive reasons. In fact, repression will reduce citizens' cooperation in collecting tax revenue and, as a consequence, property and trade taxes as well as seigniorage and state-owned enterprises will turn out to be the main revenue sources in non-democratic countries.

NOTES

1. Many of these determinant factors will be used as control variables in our empirical analysis on the level and the structure of taxation (see Chapter 3).
2. The authors underline that this is true in a relative sense, since many democracies are far from being characterized by perfect political equality because of lobbying and bribery.
3. In a non-democracy the elites have the *de jure* political power, but not necessarily the *de facto* political power too. In fact, the citizens, who are the majority and who are out of the political system, can generate social unrest and pose a revolutionary threat in order to change the future distribution of the political power. Obviously, the masses have to be able to organize themselves and to find the right momentum for their action against the regime.
4. The trade-off between democratization, other types of concessions (the 'liberalization' in the sense of O'Donnell and Schmitter, 1986) and repression has to be considered.
5. Notice that also Boix (2003) develops a comprehensive theory of the occurrence of democracy based on the distribution of income and the nature of economic assets and on the political balance of power among different social groups (see also Moore, 1966 and Webbert, 1991).
6. According to Przeworski *et al.* (2000) democratic transition would instead occur randomly (i.e. for reasons unrelated to the level of economic development), but countries with higher levels of GDP per worker would more easily remain democratic.
7. If an organizational capacity of the poor is needed, then left-wing parties and unions may be instrumental to the success of the democracy (Boix, 2003).
8. See also Boix (2003).
9. The relationship between trade and democracy depends on the distribution of factors in the economy. In countries where the poor (labour) are the abundant factor (i.e. less developed nations still far from democracy), trade openness equalizes conditions and favours the introduction of democracy. On the contrary, if the poor are the scarce factor, trade openness intensifies social conflict and raises the probability of authoritarianism (see Boix, 2003 and Acemoglu and Robinson, 2006).
10. The 'snowballing' effect which leads to a democratic contagion (Huntington, 1991).
11. In particular, Boix (2003) finds that higher levels of human capital contribute to the democratization process. Agricultural societies do not seem to affect the democratic transition but they increase the probability of democratic breakdowns. The presence of an oil economy reduces the possibilities of democratization, in this way accommodating the paradox of wealthy dictatorship. Finally, the diversification of productive activities either raises the likelihood of a democratic transition or reduces the likelihood of a democratic breakdown.
12. The authors test the modernization hypothesis starting from the result of Przeworski *et al.* (2000) according to which an increase in per capita income does not lead to a transition to democracy. Higher levels of GDP per worker are important only for a country to remain democratic.

The political economy of taxation

13. Within the colonies, the former possessions of Britain and Spain would favour democratization.
14. See also Djankov *et al.* (2003).
15. The empirical analysis of Boix (2003) shows that electoral rules do not matter for the stability of a democratic political system, while presidentialism in less developed countries may generally increase the likelihood of transition from a democracy to an autocracy. On the form of central government and the method of election in a democratic constitution, see also Shin (1994).
16. Linz (1978), Linz and Stepan (1978), O'Donnell and Schmitter (1986), Shin (1994) and Colomer (2000), among others, emphasize two different ways to democracy: the structural and the strategic process approach, in which choices and interaction by the actors play the most important role in determining the political change.
17. These results cannot be symmetrically applied to autocracies. In fact, higher income does not make autocracies less stable. More instability of autocracy also has a negative effect on growth. Even if democratic capital reduces the probability of transition away from democracy and increases the probability of exit from autocracy, the positive effect of democratic capital on growth is due only to democracy.
18. However, under a dictatorship growth is more labour extensive and labour exploitative than under a democracy. And in a non-democracy the birth rates are higher owing to higher fertility (Przeworski *et al.,* 2000).
19. Country fixed effects remove the influence of long-run factors influencing both democracy and income or education and the results of the instrumental variable (IV) approach do not show causal effect of income on democracy.
20. With reference to the sample of former European colonies, Acemoglu *et al.* (2005) show that fixed effects explaining the mentioned cross-sectional correlation are related to these historical variables such as settler mortality rates, the density of the indigenous population before colonization, the constraint on the executive at independence and the date of independence.
21. According to the authors this is the case for trade reforms in the Republic of Korea and Taiwan in the 1960s, in Chile in the 1970s, and in Turkey in the 1980s.
22. Democracies develop when the levels of inequality are moderate. As a consequence, the fiscal burden on high-income earners will not be too heavy.
23. The role of voluntary compliance has been underlined also by Wintrobe (1990), de Juan et al. (1994), Alm (1996), Pommerehne and Weck-Hannemann (1996) and Feld and Frey (2002).

3. Data, approach and overview

Our first aim is to understand what economic and political factors matter for tax revenue and tax structure. Therefore, in this chapter we provide an overview of the economic and political variables which may play a role in explaining the level of tax revenue, as well as the tax composition. For this introductory analysis, unless differently specified, we will look at data of our complete sample of new EU member countries (Cyprus, the Czech Republic, Estonia, Hungary, Latvia, Lithuania, Poland, Slovakia and Slovenia), Asian countries (China, India, Indonesia, the Republic of Korea, Malaysia, Pakistan, the Philippines, Singapore, Sri Lanka, Thailand and Vietnam) and Latin American countries (Argentina, Bolivia, Brazil, Chile, Colombia, Costa Rica, the Dominican Republic, Ecuador, El Salvador, Guatemala, Haiti, Honduras, Mexico, Nicaragua, Panama, Paraguay, Peru, Uruguay and Venezuela).[1] In particular, we will refer to new EU member countries as a benchmark of stable, though young, democracies which have recently completed their democratic transition. As such, they are particularly useful for the comparison with Asian and Latin American areas, where democracy is much more unstable even in recent years. The preliminary evidence presented in this chapter motivates the specific focus of analysis that these two areas will receive in Chapters 4 and 5.

We will compare our preliminary evidence with the directions of the relationships predicted by the theoretical studies and with the findings of other empirical works on taxation, in particular those which focus on developing countries.

We will first adopt a parsimonious baseline specification where we introduce only what are considered the fundamental economic and political variables associated with tax revenue and then include additional control variables and perform robustness check analysis. Then we will turn to tax structure and we will study how these fundamental economic and political variables are associated with some specific features of tax design and tax composition.

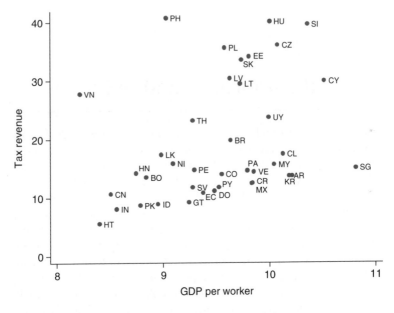

Note: See list of abbrevations in Appendix at the end of chapter.

Figure 3.1   Tax revenue and GDP per worker

3.1   THE ECONOMIC FUNDAMENTALS

The first economic variable is a measure of the development of the economy which we typically proxy by GDP per worker and the growth rate of real GDP per capita. This is expected to be positively correlated with tax revenue. Figure 3.1 shows this positive association for our sample of countries using average values of tax revenue and GDP per worker for the considered period (1990–2004).[2]

This positive relation is consistent with the idea that the ability to tax grows faster than income. A large literature has studied the evolution of tax revenue with the level of economic development (see Hinrichs, 1966; Tanzi, 1992). Musgrave (1969) argues that the lack of availability of 'tax handles' might limit revenue collection at low levels of income and these limitations should become less severe as the economy develops. Moreover, according to Wagner's law, economic development is associated with an increased demand for

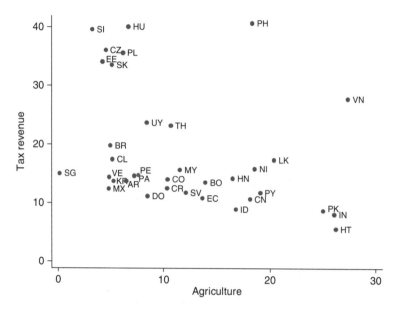

Note: See list of abbrevations in Appendix at the end of chapter.

Figure 3.2   Tax revenue and agriculture

public expenditure (Tanzi, 1987). Not only does economic development widen the tax base, but it also improves administrative capacity to levy and collect taxes (Chelliah, 1971). All these mechanisms
should thus result in a positive relationship between GDP per
worker and tax revenue.

Following Burgess and Stern (1993) and Gupta (2007), we then
turn to three other fundamental economic determinants of the share
of tax revenue over GDP: the share of agriculture over GDP, the
openness of the economy as a percentage of GDP and the debt/GDP
ratio.[3]

Figure 3.2 shows for our sample of countries a negative association between tax revenue and the share of agriculture in GDP.[4] A
country's economic structure is one of the main elements that may
influence the level of taxation, since some sectors of the economy are
easier to tax than others. For developing countries, the share of agriculture is predicted to be negatively related to the level of tax revenue
(Tanzi, 1992; Ghura, 1998). The reason is twofold. On the supply

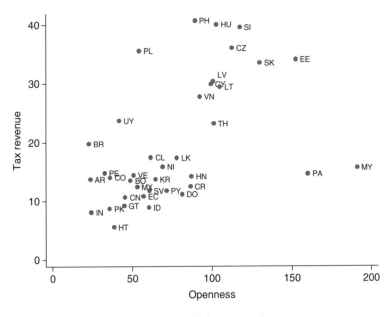

Note: See list of abbrevations in Appendix at the end of chapter.

Figure 3.3   Tax revenue and openness

side, it is very difficult to tax the agricultural sector 'explicitly', though it is often very heavily taxed in many implicit ways such as import quotas, tariffs, controlled prices for output, or overvalued exchange rates (Bird, 1974; Ahmad and Stern, 1991; Tanzi, 1992). This is because small farmers are notoriously difficult to tax, and a large share of agriculture is normally subsistence, which does not generate large taxable surpluses, as many countries are unwilling to tax the main foods that are used for subsistence (Stotsky and WoldeMariam, 1997). On the demand side, since many public sector activities are largely city oriented, the more agricultural a country is, the less it will have to spend for governmental activities and services. Hence, as the share of agriculture over GDP rises, the need for total public spending and so for tax revenue may fall.

Figure 3.3 shows the relationship between tax revenue and openness in our sample of countries. The openness of the economy is another important determinant of the level of tax revenue. Trade-related taxes (imports and exports) are easier to impose because they

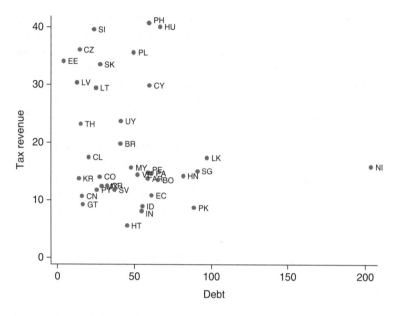

Note: See list of abbrevations in Appendix at the end of chapter.

Figure 3.4   Tax revenue and debt

take place at specified locations. Moreover, since more open economies are exposed to more external risks, citizens will demand a larger
role of government in providing social insurance to protect against
these risks (Rodrik, 1998). Thus, a positive correlation between trade
openness and tax revenue will emerge.

In developing countries the prediction on the sign of this relationship is ambiguous: on one hand the trade liberalization which took
place in the 1990s may have induced a reduction in tariffs, which has
in turn decreased this source of tax revenue, while on the other hand,
if trade liberalization occurs through tariffication of quotas, elimina-
tions of exemptions, reduction in tariff peaks and improvement in
customs procedures, revenue may even increase with openness (Keen
and Simone, 2004).

Finally, Figure 3.4 shows the relationship between tax revenue
and debt in our sample of countries, which appears quite flat. The
level of debt of a country may indeed affect revenue. The growth of
public spending has generated large fiscal deficits in many countries,

leading to increases in the share of public debt relative to GDP. With a large debt, the government needs to raise the revenue necessary to service it. When the interest on the debt exceeds net borrowing plus the possible reduction in non-interest expenditure, taxes should rise, unless the growth rate of the economy is high enough to compensate. Therefore 'public debt plays a role in determining the extent to which countries may take advantage of their taxable capacity' (Tanzi, 1987). In general, a high debt will require high tax revenue *ceteris paribus* (Tanzi, 1992). Notice however that a high debt can also create macroeconomic imbalances that may tend to reduce the tax level: countries faced with an increased trade deficit may for instance try to restrict imports, and thus revenue from import duties will decrease with a negative impact on the overall tax revenue.

3.2   THE POLITICAL FUNDAMENTALS

3.2.1   Measures of Democracy

There is a great deal of debate among political scientists on how to measure democracy, because the definition of what constitutes a democracy is not uncontroversial. The definition proposed by Schumpeter (1942) is generally accepted as a reference starting point: 'democracy is the institutional arrangement for arriving at political decisions in which individuals acquire the power to decide by means of a competitive struggle for the people's vote'. This definition suggests that democracy is identified by specific institutions, which guarantee free and fair elections, the accountability of politicians to the electorate and free entry in politics. However, how to measure these institutional conditions is neither obvious nor uncontroversial. Scholars and political scientists are divided between those who consider the best correspondence to this definition of democracy to be a simple dichotomous classification, that is a country is either democratic or not (Przeworski *et al.*, 2000), and those who develop a continuous measure of democracy based on a specific index. It is out of our scope to solve this controversy. While we consider the dichotomous classification useful, especially when a transition is analysed, in this book we will mainly refer to continuous measures of democracy, which allows us to capture more features of a political regime and to better address cross-country differences. We will thus concentrate on three main continuous measures of democracy, given by the Polity IV dataset and the Freedom House.

First, we use data from the Polity IV dataset (2007), which contains an indicator called POLITY2, computed for a very large number of countries by subtracting an annual measure of institutionalized autocracy (AUTOC) from an annual measure of institutionalized democracy (DEMOC), both ranging from 0 to 10. These measures are constructed by taking into account the competitiveness of political participation, the regulation of participation, the openness and competitiveness of executive recruitment and the constraints on the chief executive that characterize a specific country. As a consequence, the POLITY2 score ranges from −10 (strong autocracy) to +10 (strong democracy). In particular, DEMOC is a measure for institutionalized democracy and is conceived of as three essential and interdependent elements: (i) the presence of institutions and procedures through which citizens can express effectively their preferences about alternative policies and leaders, (ii) substantial institutionalized constraints on the exercise of power by the executive, and (iii) the guarantee of civil liberties to all citizens in their daily lives and in acts of political participation (although they are not actually measured). The rule of laws, systems of checks and balances, freedom of the press, and other aspects of democracies are included, because they are considered specific means of these three elements. AUTOC is a measure for institutionalized autocracies, that is political systems whose common features are a lack of regularized political competition and concern for political freedoms. Both the indicators range from 0 to 10 and are derived from coding of the competitiveness of political participation, the openness and competitiveness of executive recruitment, and constraints on the chief executive using different weights.

Though we will also consider separately the indicators of democracy (DEMOC) and autocracy (AUTOC) throughout the analysis, the POLITY2 indicator will be the most important political variable, since it allows simultaneous consideration of the level of democracy and the level of autocracy in a particular country. In fact a higher level of the POLITY2 indicator can be alternatively read as a higher level of democracy, the level of autocracy being equal, or a lower level of autocracy, the level of democracy being equal.

The Polity IV dataset (2007) also provides information on the duration of the polity regime (DURABLE). Starting from this, we construct an additive variable DUR_POLITY (DURABLE x

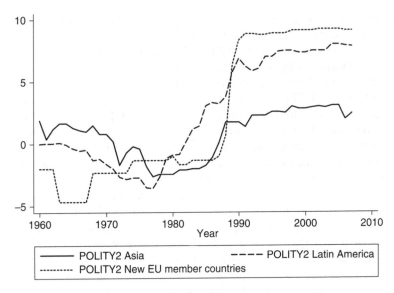

Figure 3.5   The evolution of POLITY2

POLITY) to measure the interaction between the political regime and its duration. This variable may capture interesting insights into the relationship, if any, of a long-lasting democracy, as opposed to a long-lasting autocracy, to taxation.

The second source of political variables is the Freedom House which includes two alternative measures of democratization: the first one is called civil liberties (FREEDOM1) and is measured on a 1-to-7 scale, with 1 representing the highest degree of freedom of expression, organization, assembly, property rights protection and equality under the law and 7 the lowest. Notice that a higher score of FREEDOM1 corresponds to a lower level of democracy. The second indicator of Freedom House is called political rights (FREEDOM2) and is conceived of as rights that enable people to participate freely in the political process; in particular it is related to the existence of free and fair elections, the right to organize, the existence of a credible opposition, the avoidance of corruption and similar rights. It is again measured on a 1-to-7 scale, with 1 representing the highest degree of freedom and 7 the lowest.

Figure 3.5 shows the evolution of democracy in the three areas at the centre of our analysis using the POLITY2 indicator. We look at the average indexes of democracy in countries belonging to each of the considered areas from the 1960s. Notice that in all areas there is a general increasing trend towards democracy in the period that we analyse (1990–2004). Considering a longer span, dating back to the 1960s, democracy declined in particular in Latin America in the 1970s. Substantial increases of the POLITY2 indicator began in the 1980s in all areas. The new EU members entered the 1980s with their indicators aligned with those of the other countries and overtook the others in the following 20 years, with a much more abrupt change in the late 1980s.

Though these average patterns are interesting for showing some common regularity and making initial comparisons, the large amount of heterogeneity within each area requires a more disaggregated and detailed analysis. We will turn to this in Chapters 4 and 5, where we will analyse Asia and Latin America separately.

3.2.2 Democracy and Income

As explained in Chapter 2, Lipset (1959) argued that rich countries tend to be more democratic.

Figures 3.6a and 3.6b follow this intuition and show the positive correlation between GDP per worker and our measures of democracy for our countries: in Figure 3.6a we plot the average POLITY2 index for the period 1990–2004 for our countries versus the average log of GDP for the same period, and in Figure 3.6b we use the Freedom House indicator of civil liberties (FREEDOM1[5]) instead of the POLITY2 one. Richer countries are more democratic than poorer ones. On the role of this positive correlation between income and democracy as formalized by the well-known modernization theory we direct readers back to Chapter 2.

We emphasize that the correlations shown in Figures 3.6a and 3.6b are not meant to capture causal effects, that is that as a country becomes richer it will certainly adopt a more democratic institution. Other historical and institutional factors may influence both the economic and the political development paths of different societies, as argued by Acemoglu *et al.* (2004, 2005).

To limit this causality and omitted variables problem, we will restrict our analysis by considering separately each of the specific areas of developing countries. Obviously, this is not meant to be a complete solution, but to control for the heterogeneity which may

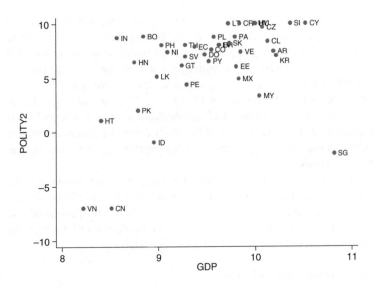

Note: See list of abbrevations in Appendix at the end of chapter.

Figure 3.6a   Political variables and GDP: POLITY2

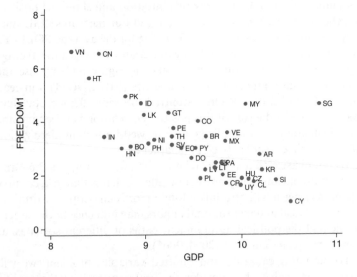

Note: See list of abbrevations in Appendix at the end of chapter.

Figure 3.6b   Political variables and GDP: FREEDOM1

arise not only within countries in each of the areas of our sample but also across areas.

Before analysing the relationship between democracy and taxation we should also have a look at the link between democracy and inequality, since taxation is the main tool to realize income redistribution. To measure inequality we use the Gini index.

Figures 3.7a and 3.7b show the correlations between the Gini index and, respectively, the POLITY2 and the FREEDOM1 (civil liberties) indexes of democracy. The relation seems quite weak, though slightly positive between the level of inequality and indicators of democracy.

Many authors have argued that democracy is not possible in very unequal societies (Dahl, 1971). The empirical literature has however not reached a consensus on the sign of this relationship (see Lichbach, 1989 for a review). Bollen and Jackman (1985) found that there is no relationship between democracy and inequality; others have argued that inequality may even stabilize dictatorships (Muller, 1995) or it may create an obstacle to the democratization process (Boix, 2003), while Alesina and Perotti have stressed that inequality may increase political instability. Przeworski *et al.* (2000) found that the relation between inequality and democracy may depend on how we measure inequality. If inequality is measured by the Gini coefficient, or by the ratio between the income of the top 10 per cent of the population in the distribution of income and the bottom 10 per cent, inequality has no impact on the probability of democratization, while, if it is measured by the share of income in manufacturing that accrues to workers, higher inequality is associated with higher instability, both of dictatorships and of democracies. Therefore, our result that there is almost no relation between inequality measured by the Gini index and political variables is in line with these predictions.

3.2.3 Democracy and Taxation

The relationship between redistributive policies and democracies has been analysed within the political economy literature (see Chapter 2). However, the attention paid to the design and structure of the tax system has been quite limited so far.

Many have argued that democracy and the duration of democratic institutions are associated with more tax revenue, while autocracy

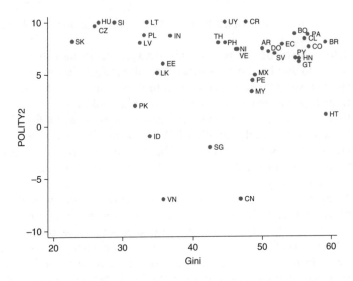

Note: See list of abbrevations in Appendix at the end of chapter.

Figure 3.7a   Political variables and inequality: POLITY2

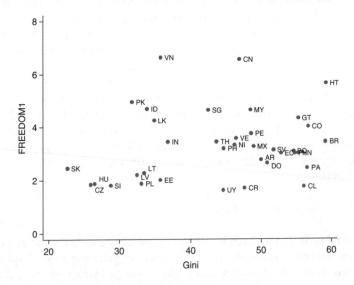

Note: See list of abbrevations in Appendix at the end of chapter.

Figure 3.7b   Political variables and inequality: FREEDOM1

goes in the opposite direction. The crucial intuition is that under a non-democratic regime the size of the public sector and of redistributive spending is small, since a substantial part of the electorate is excluded from the decision-making process. A transition to democracy, on the contrary, should raise taxes and public spending, since democratization will involve demands for government to assume more responsibility for the unemployed, sick, poor and elderly. Other studies however have argued that the empirical evidence does not confirm this result and that indeed democracies do not redistribute more than non-democracies (Mulligan *et al.*, 2004).

To solve the controversy is out of the scope of this work: we focus here only on a sample of developing countries which is interesting for the analysis of the relationship between democracy and taxation, but not enough for establishing the sign of the controversial relationship.

The preliminary evidence reported in Figures 3.8a and 3.8b suggests that there exists a positive correlation between the democratic performance of the countries, as captured by both the POLITY2 and the FREEDOM1 (civil liberties) indicators, and the share of tax revenue over GDP. These correlations should not be interpreted as a causal relationship, but they represent a reference framework for our analysis in the next chapters. In our baseline specification we will combine economic and political variables to provide a first broader view of what is related to tax revenue.

3.3   AN ENRICHED SCENARIO

Other policies may be important in governments' tax revenue collection and in their attempts to influence the distribution of income in the society (see Di Nardo *et al.*, 1996), such as those related to education, pensions and the labour market. Moreover, other demographic and economic factors may play a relevant role to determine the level of tax revenue, for example the education level of the population, the share of elderley people, the female labour force participation, and also the urbanization process, the density of the population and the size of the shadow economy.

Plotting a measure of the number of years of secondary schooling attainment by the population and the political measures gives interesting correlations (see Figures 3.9a and 3.9b): more educated

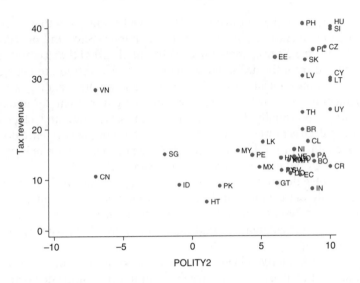

Note: See list of abbrevations in Appendix at the end of chapter.

Figure 3.8a   Political variables and tax revenue: POLITY2

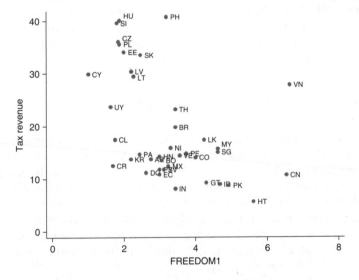

Note: See list of abbrevations in Appendix at the end of chapter.

Figure 3.8b   Political variables and tax revenue: FREEDOM1

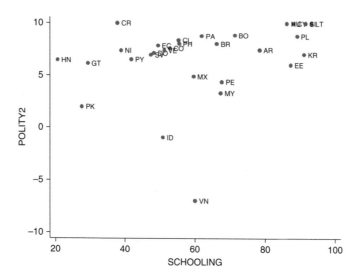

Note: See list of abbreviations in Appendix at the end of chapter.

Figure 3.9a   Political variables and schooling: POLITY2

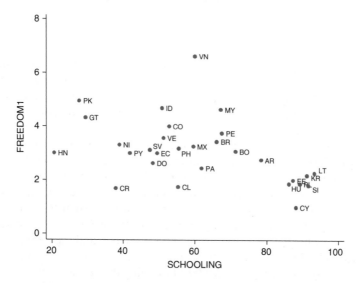

Note: See list of abbreviations in Appendix at the end of chapter.

Figure 3.9b   Political variables and schooling: FREEDOM1

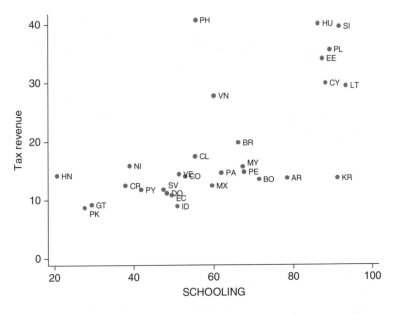

Figure 3.10   Tax revenue and schooling

countries tend to be more democratic (see also Chapter 2). Since education is typically a good proxy of income, education may also be important in contributing to explaining the level of tax revenue (see section 3.1 and Figure 3.10). We will thus use it as a control variable when explaining the level of tax revenue.

Another crucial policy is pension. Pension expenditure represents the largest share of government expenditure as a percentage of GDP in many developed countries. In developing countries, the pension system is instead a great challenge. Many countries that we analyse have a very embryonic social security system (China, for instance). However, under the pressures of the ageing of the population together with the urbanization phenomenon and the weakening of family ties, pensions will become an essential source of old age income (see Galasso *et al.*, 2009). Enlarging the pension system will be a top priority for the policy makers of these countries. This welfare expenditure will need to be financed by an increase of tax revenue and therefore we should expect, at least in the future, a positive rela-

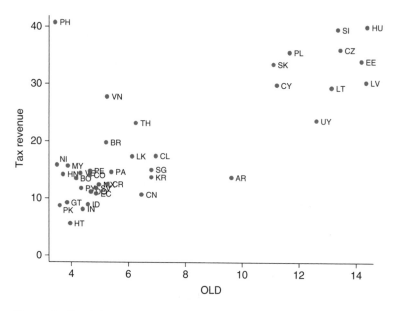

Note: See list of abbrevations in Appendix at the end of chapter.

Figure 3.11 Tax revenue and the share of people over 65 in the population

tionship between the percentage of elderly in the population and the level of tax revenue. However, it may also be the case that more aged societies are able to collect less tax revenue owing to a more limited labour force participation. This negative relation between the share of elderly in the population and tax revenue may prevail in countries where the pensions system is currently still very limited (Asian countries, for instance). Thus, the final relation may be ambiguous.

For our sample of countries the relationship between the level of tax revenue and the share of people over 65 in the population seems to be positive (Figure 3.11), although we should notice that, restricting the attention to the Asian area, it tends to be negative.

Another relevant variable is female labour force participation; when more women are employed in the official market, tax revenue increases, as shown in Figure 3.12.

In our enriched scenario we finally control for three further potential determinants of the level of tax revenue, typically identified by the empirical literature on taxation in developing countries.

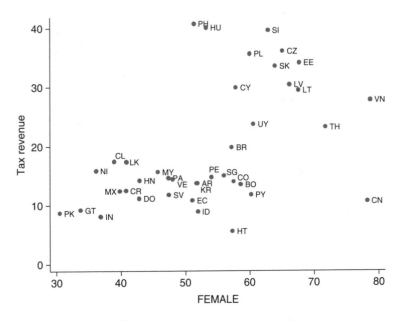

Note: See list of abbrevations in Appendix at the end of chapter.

Figure 3.12   Tax revenue and female labour force participation rate

The first one is urbanization, which increases the demand for public services, while at the same time facilitating tax collection (Tanzi, 1987). Notice that urbanization and economic development are strictly related. The positive relationship between urbanization and the level of tax revenue is shown in Figure 3.13.

Then we turn to population density: the higher the density of population the higher will be the use of taxable sources (i.e. increasing the tax base), and the tax authorities could intensify their efforts to collect taxes at a relatively minimal cost as compared to the case in a sparsely populated country. Conversely, in a thinly populated area, administrative costs are expected to be higher in terms of total yields and therefore less encouraging for the collection of tax revenues. In such a situation, the degree of tax evasion and tax avoidance may also be relatively higher than in a densely populated area (Ansari, 1982).

Finally, a measure of the informal or shadow economy is typically considered one of the determinants of tax revenue. A large literature has analysed the relationship between the shadow economy and

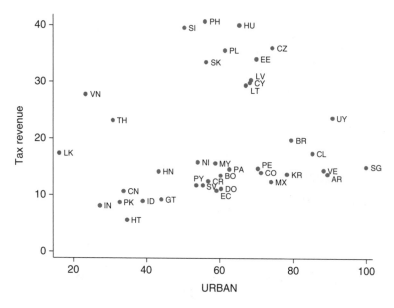

Note: See list of abbrevations in Appendix at the end of chapter.

Figure 3.13   Tax revenue and urbanization

tax revenue: since higher taxes strengthen the incentives to work in the black market, the underground economy increases with the tax burden (e.g. Allingham and Sandmo, 1972). The bigger the difference between the total cost of labour in the official economy and the after-tax earnings (from work), the greater is the incentive to avoid this difference and to work in the shadow economy. Since this difference depends broadly on the social security burden/payments and the overall tax burden, the latter are key features of the existence and the increase of the shadow economy (Schneider, 2005, 2007).

Many empirical studies have provided support for this positive relationship between tax revenue and the shadow economy: in Johnson *et al.* (1998a, 1998b) the tax burden is cited as one of the three main causes of the underground economy; Schneider and Enste (2000) argue that taxes, together with the state regulatory activities, are the most important determinants behind the growth of the hidden economy; using data for Canada, Giles and Tedds (2002) find a clear and significant statistical evidence of two-way Granger causality, both from the effective tax rate to the underground

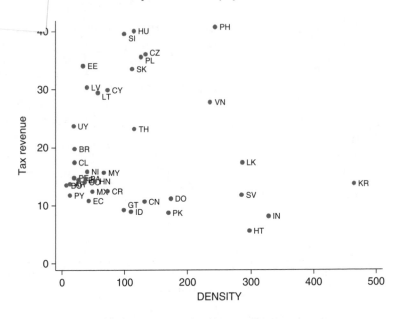

Notes:
1. See list of abbreviations in Appendix at the end of chapter.
2. Singapore is excluded from the sample, because it is an outlier.

Figure 3.14   Tax revenue and population density

economy and from the underground economy to the effective tax rate. Schneider (1994, 2000, 2005) and Johnson *et al.* (1998a, 1998b) found statistically significant evidence for the influence of taxation on the shadow economy (see also Thomas, 1992; Lippert and Walker, 1997).

Tanzi (1999) argues that the large increase of the level of taxation and tax rates of the last few decades (Tanzi and Schuknecht, 1997) has created strong incentives for individuals and enterprises to go 'underground' to avoid taxes – in particular income taxes, value added taxes and social security taxes – and regulatory restrictions.

Shadow economies characterize to an important extent all types of economies: developing, transition and highly developed OECD countries. In all these countries, taxes (both direct and indirect) are the driving forces of the growth of the shadow economy, followed by the measure of state (labour market) regulation and, as measures of the official economy, the unemployment quota and GDP per

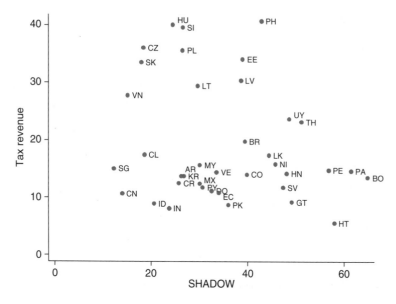

Note: See list of abbrevations in Appendix at the end of chapter.

Figure 3.15   Tax revenue and the size of the shadow economy

capita. However, in developing countries the burden of state regulation has the largest influence, followed by the unemployment quota
and the share of indirect taxation. In the transition countries direct
taxation (including social security payments) plays the most important role, followed by the unemployment quota and share of indirect
taxation. In the highly developed OECD countries, the social security
contributions and the share of direct taxation wield the biggest influence, followed by tax morale and the quality of state institutions.

3.4   TAX DESIGN AND COMPOSITION

We now turn to tax design and composition and see how the fundamental economic and political variables are associated with the
specific features of tax structure.

First evidence is reported in Figures 3.16 to 3.20 using as indicators of democracy POLITY2 and FREEDOM1 (civil liberties).

Figures 3.16a and 3.16b show a positive association between the

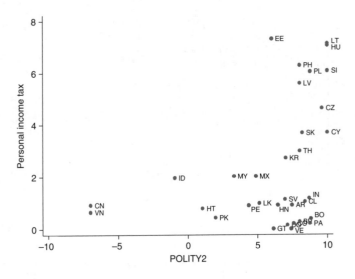

Note: See list of abbreviations in Appendix at the end of chapter.

Figure 3.16a   Personal income tax and democracy: POLITY2

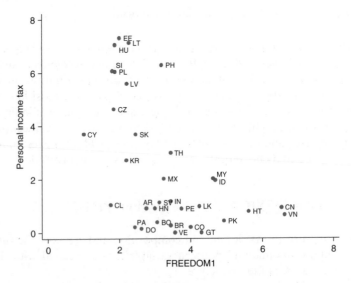

Note: See list of abbreviations in Appendix at the end of chapter.

Figure 3.16b   Personal income tax and democracy: FREEDOM1

level of personal income taxes and democracy, while the relation with corporate income taxes is much less clear (Figures 3.17a and 3.17b). In particular, it seems that countries are grouped by areas, which justifies why a detailed analysis for each world's area is recommended. This suggestion is confirmed by looking at the total amount of direct taxes in Figures 3.18a and 3.18b. While Asian and new EU member countries seem to confirm the positive association between direct taxes and a democratic regime, Latin American ones drive the 'flat' part of the plot, that is they seem to show no relation with our indicators of democracy. Since direct taxes are at the core of government redistributive policies, this result needs a deeper analysis, which we will develop in the next chapters.

As for indirect taxes, Figures 3.19a and 3.19b show the relationship between the level of taxes on goods and services as a percentage of GDP and two of our indicators of democracy. Again, this evidence has a difficult interpretation: the relation seems to be positive, although countries of different areas are grouped together. In other words, it seems that the sign of the relation is not unaltered when restricting our attention to a specific world area.

The literature has developed several ideas on the tax mix in democratic versus autocratic countries (see Chapter 2). Musgrave (1969) argues that, since one of the main goals of individual taxation is to redistribute income or realize some social goal, more autocratic countries, which directly exercise more control on the economy in general, and on wages in particular, do not need this source of taxation. They instead rely more on corporate taxation, mainly state enterprise in socialist countries, for instance, or even private business, for ideological reasons. This is however not consistent with the result in Mulligan *et al.* (2004), who find that income tax structures are flatter in democracies than in non-democracies, which implies that redistribution is not more important in democracies than in non-democracies. An alternative explanation of the different tax mix in democratic versus autocratic countries is also offered by Wintrobe (1990), who suggests that, since democratic countries do not use repressive measures as governing instruments, they have to design tax systems that induce more voluntary tax compliance (see also de Juan *et al.*, 1994; Alm 1996; Pommerehne and Weck-Hannemann 1996; Feld and Frey 2002). Mature democracies thus rely more on revenue sources, such as self-assessed personal income taxation, based on voluntary tax compliance, while more repressive governments that cannot rely on

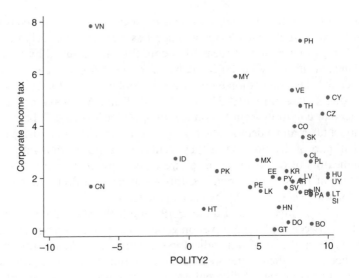

Note: See list of abbrevations in Appendix at the end of chapter.

Figure 3.17a   Corporate income tax and democracy: POLITY2

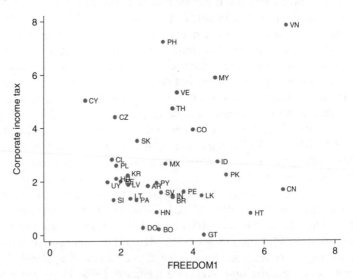

Note: See list of abbrevations in Appendix at the end of chapter.

Figure 3.17b   Corporate income tax and democracy: FREEDOM1

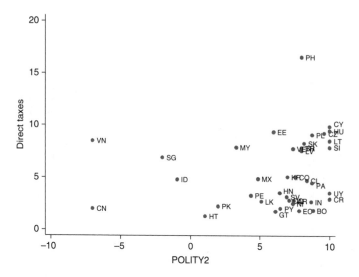

Note: See list of abbreviations in Appendix at the end of chapter.

Figure 3.18a   Direct taxes and democracy: POLITY2

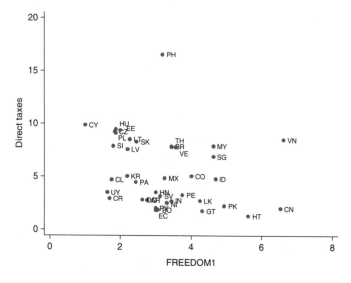

Note: See list of abbreviations in Appendix at the end of chapter.

Figure 3.18b   Direct taxes and democracy: FREEDOM1

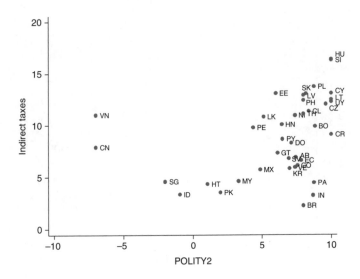

Note: See list of abbreviations in Appendix at the end of chapter.

Figure 3.19a   Indirect taxes and democracy: POLITY2

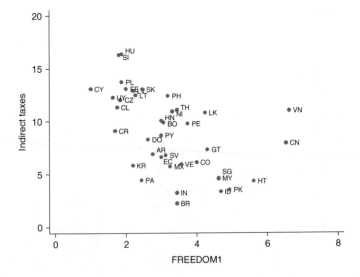

Note: See list of abbreviations in Appendix at the end of chapter.

Figure 3.19b   Indirect taxes and democracy: FREEDOM1

tax sources requiring a certain level of voluntary cooperation, such as personal income taxes, move toward corporate taxes or trade taxes.

Our results are to some extent consistent with these different findings of the literature. For the Latin American area, as in Mulligan *et al.* (2004), we could not find a relationship between the level of democratization and the level of direct, redistributive, taxes. For the Asian area the tax mix seems to associate more democracy with more direct taxes (Musgrave, 1969). A detailed discussion will be provided in the following chapters.

Social security is also a policy which may entail redistributive features. Figures 3.20a and 3.20b show the relation between the level of social security contributions and our democratic indicators. The figures suggest that in these countries the relationship is not as strong as predicted by the political economy literature based on the median voter's theorem. Instead there is almost no relationship between the extension of social security and the level of democracy, closer to the findings of Mulligan *et al.* (2004).

Finally, the other sources of tax revenue (mainly property and trade taxes) do not show a clear relation with our political indicators, and thus, lacking an interpretation, we have decided not to report the related figures.

3.5 CONCLUSIONS

This chapter has provided an overview of the relationships between what we have called fundamental economic variables and the level of tax revenue, as well as tax structure and design in our sample of countries belonging to the new EU members, Asian and Latin American areas for the average of the period 1990–2004. We have also looked at three different measures of democracy and at additional economic variables which may play a role in explaining tax revenue and tax structure.

Our findings suggest that tax revenue may be indeed positively related with democracy, that is more democratic countries tend to have a higher level of tax revenue. However, when turning to the analysis of the tax structure, the cross-country evidence is quite mixed and ambiguous and it seems difficult to predict relations. Though more democracy turns out to be associated with more personal income taxes, nothing certain can be said on the tax mix of

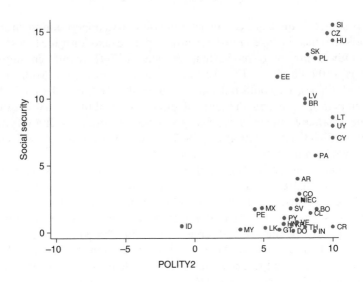

Note: See list of abbreviations in Appendix at the end of chapter.

Figure 3.20a   Social security and democracy: POLITY2

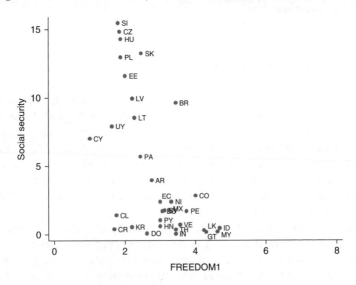

Note: See list of abbreviations in Appendix at the end of chapter.

Figure 3.20b   Social security and democracy: FREEDOM1

direct versus indirect taxes, since indirect taxes also seem to be larger in more democratic contexts. Social security contributions appear not to be related with the level of democracy. A possible reconciliation of this result with the theoretical predictions that more democracy should be associated with more redistribution (mainly attained through direct taxes and social security) is that many developing countries also use indirect taxes with some redistributive purpose.

However we consider this evidence too unclear to draw conclusions. The specific economic and political context of each area matters. Thus, we should analyse the specific areas, as we will do in the next chapters.

NOTES

1. Our complete sample includes all the countries that joined the European Union in 2004, except for Malta due to lack of data; a set of developing countries that are well representative of the three main regions of the Asian Continent (Far East, South and East, and the Indian sub-continent) and a reasonable set of Latin American transition countries.
2. In all the figures of this chapter we build the average of the plotted variables for the period 1990–2004.
3. See also our discussion on additional control variables in section 3.3.
4. Notice however that data on agriculture referring to the different areas may be difficult to compare, owing to source heterogeneity. In Figure 3.2 we have excluded new EU member countries, since the share of agriculture is calculated there as a percentage of GDP rather than of value added (OECD, 2008).
5. The two indicators of Freedom House, FREEDOM1 and FREEDOM 2, show quite similar patterns and thus we have decided to report figures using only FREEDOM1.

APPENDIX TO CHAPTER 3:
LIST OF ABBREVIATIONS

AR	Argentina	LT	Lithuania
BO	Bolivia	LV	Latvia
BR	Brazil	MX	Mexico
CL	Chile	MY	Malaysia
CN	China	NI	Nicaragua
CO	Colombia	PA	Panama
CR	Costa Rica	PE	Peru
CY	Cyprus	PH	Philippines
CZ	Czech Republic	PK	Pakistan
DO	Dominican Republic	PL	Poland
EC	Ecuador	PY	Paraguay
EE	Estonia	SG	Singapore
GT	Guatemala	SI	Slovenia
HN	Honduras	SK	Slovakia
HT	Haiti	SV	El Salvador
HU	Hungary	TH	Thailand
ID	Indonesia	UY	Uruguay
IN	India	VE	Venezuala
KR	Republic of Korea	VN	Vietnam
LK	Sri Lanka		

4. Asia

4.1 INTRODUCTION

This chapter focuses on a sample of Asian countries including China, India, Indonesia, the Republic of Korea, Malaysia, Pakistan, the Philippines, Singapore, Sri Lanka, Thailand and Vietnam. Given the magnitude of the Asian continent, we consider these countries representative of its three main regions: Far East, South and East, and Indian sub-continent.

We start from the observation that most of these countries have a low fiscal pressure and a 'light' welfare state (Jacobs, 1998). Tax revenue as a percentage of GDP in 2004 was lower than 20 per cent in China, India, Indonesia, the Republic of Korea, Singapore and Malaysia, among others (IMF, 2006, see Data Appendix in Chapter 7), though on an increasing path. Welfare expenditures were also very low. In 2004, the level of public health expenditure, for instance, was 0.4 per cent of GDP in Pakistan, reaching 3 per cent of GDP only in the Republic of Korea (WDI, 2007, see Data Appendix in Chapter 7).[1] In many of these countries enterprises and families have traditionally played a major welfare role and have partially compensated for the low public spending. In some countries, enterprises have adopted a variety of flexibility measures to keep workers who are not necessarily profitable, while in other Asian countries three-generation families substitute for the public welfare system by pooling income between workers and economically inactive people. The quasi-absence of the welfare state is also based on the common practice that women are the main providers of personal care for children and the elderly at home.

The interrelated low fiscal pressure and 'light' welfare state are however under challenge. Asian countries, especially China and Singapore, are growing fast and their economic and social development should urgently require a rethinking of the welfare and fiscal policies. On the expenditure side, in these countries the forms of enterprise and family welfare are currently being challenged by socio-economic conditions, in particular the financial crisis (which has substantially raised unemployment, for instance in the Republic of Korea), falling fertility and the ageing process (in China and Thailand, but also in the Republic of Korea), as well as by some other common trends, such as urbanization, the passage from enlarged to single family unit and the rise of female employment (which imply a reduced readiness of women to care for their parents or children). The World Bank (1999) identifies 'social protection' as a strategic sector for the structural long-term development of Asian countries. This sector includes three areas, strictly interrelated: social safety nets (including social funds), labour market policies (including child labour) and pensions. This last area, pensions, is crucial, especially for countries in which the demographic transition is well advanced, such as China, Thailand and the Republic of Korea. As a consequence, welfare expenditure is expected to increase in Asian countries as well as the level of tax revenue. Moreover, crucial challenges for fiscal reforms are the introduction of a more modern fiscal structure, based on the simplification of tax administration, the fight against fiscal evasion and the development of fiscal decentralization. These innovations will realistically contribute to raise fiscal pressure.

Although these countries are facing common demographic and socio-economic trends, they are equipped with quite different political regimes. Some countries show a tradition of high democracy and some others either show a trend to democratization only in recent years or are characterized by non-democratic institutions. In particular, according to our data, the countries with the highest levels of democracy are India, the Republic of Korea, the Philippines and, to a lesser extent, Sri Lanka and Malaysia ('old democracies'). Thailand and Indonesia instead showed a trend to democratization only in the early and late 1990s respectively ('young democracies'). Conversely, China, Vietnam and Singapore are traditional non-democratic countries in which communist parties play the most important role in politics ('non-democracies'). Finally, Pakistan changed democratic for non-democratic institutions in the late 1990s, but restored democracy in 2007. In the appendix to this chapter we will provide more details on the historical evolution of the political regimes for each analysed country.

In this chapter we investigate the potential role of the political institutions in addressing the expected changes in welfare and fiscal policies. A large theoretical and empirical literature has studied the role of democratization on redistribution (see Chapter 2). The Asian region is a very interesting case to investigate: on one hand the socio-economic changes will push towards higher taxation; on the other hand the lack of democracy may represent an obstacle to the design of modern, redistributive fiscal policies. Will the political regime be crucial to help the Asian region to cope with the necessary rethinking of redistributive policies? Are countries with opposite political regimes responding differently to the demographic and socio-economic challenges, in terms of public policies, specifically taxation?

We focus our attention on taxation by providing a positive analysis of the determinants of tax revenue and investigating the structure and composition of taxation in the period 1990–2004[2] with reference to the 11 Asian countries in our sample. In a regression analysis, we find that, in addition to standard economic variables, tax revenue as a percentage of GDP is related to political factors, such as the level of democratization of the country. Second, we emphasize the role of political regimes for tax policies and design across countries. More democratic countries have more personal income taxation and in general are associated with less indirect taxation, while more autocratic countries have more corporate income taxation.

Our results are consistent with those found in previous studies (see Chapter 2), but we have a different and new perspective: we focus only on Asian countries, but consider all their main taxes for the period 1990–2004. Since Asia is characterized by several specific features for taxation and welfare, our study, which narrows and limits its analysis to this specific area, has a double advantage with respect to previous broader studies: these specific features can emerge in a clear and more precise picture, and they can be discussed in a policy perspective appropriate to their institutional environment, quite different from that of the rest of the world.

4.2   OVERVIEW OF TAX SYSTEMS AND POLITICAL REGIMES

In this section we analyse the determinants of tax revenue in our selected sample of Asian countries for which data on taxes and political regimes are available from homogeneous sources. We explore which economic factors affect tax revenue and the level of specific

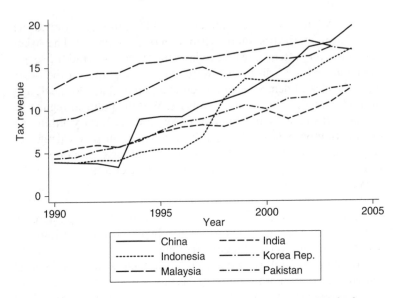

Source: Our calculations from IMF *Government Finance Statistics Yearbook*
(various years).

*Figure 4.1a   The evolution of tax revenue (percentage of GDP) in
              Asia 1990–2004*

taxes (i.e. personal income, corporate) and especially which role is
played by the political regime.

We first present a brief, not exhaustive, overview of data on
tax systems and political regimes in these countries. Asia is a fast-
developing and highly economically integrated area, but its countries
are not homogeneous (as for instance in Latin America and, to a lesser
extent, Eastern Europe). The levels of GDP per worker are very different; some countries (i.e. Singapore, the Republic of Korea, Malaysia)
are more developed, while others (i.e. Vietnam, India, Pakistan) lag
behind (Penn World Tables, 2006, see Data Appendix in Chapter 7).
Moreover, there is no supra-national authority which coordinates
single countries' policies and harmonizes their institutions.

Figures 4.1a and 4.1b show the evolution of tax revenue over
the period 1990–2004 in these countries, and Tables 4.1a and 4.1b
summarize the structure of tax revenue, comparing 1990 and 2004
data.[3]

Tax revenue is quite low, especially if compared with that of

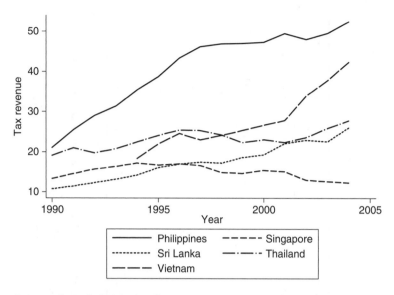

Source: Our calculations from IMF *Government Finance Statistics Yearbook* (various years).

Figure 4.1b   The evolution of tax revenue (percentage of GDP) in Asia 1990–2004

countries in other world areas with a similar per capita income (CIS countries, for example): in percentage of GDP it is, in 2004, 12.31 in Singapore, 12.59 in India, 12.79 in Pakistan, 17.79 in Indonesia, 17.39 in Malaysia and 19.8 in China (IMF, 2006, see Data Appendix in Chapter 7). Even in the Republic of Korea, an industrialized country with a per capita income similar to that of many Western European countries (such as Greece and Portugal, for instance), the tax revenue reaches only 17.01 per cent of income (34.3 per cent in Greece and 35.4 per cent in Portugal). The highest values are in Sri Lanka, Thailand, Vietnam and the Philippines: respectively 26.33, 27.75, 42.34 and 52.41 per cent of GDP.

Similarly to what happens in most developing and transition economies (Burgess and Stern, 1993), indirect taxes prevail over direct ones, with the major exceptions of Malaysia and the Philippines, and with India and Singapore showing quite similar values. A low tax wedge on labour improves efficiency, while a high burden on consumption reduces equity and induces welfare losses.

Table 4.1a *Structure of tax revenue (percentage of GDP) in Asia in 1990*

	China	India	Indonesia	Korea, Rep.	Malaysia	Pakistan	Philippines	Singapore	Sri Lanka	Thailand	Vietnam*
Tax on income, profits, capital gains	1.97	0.91	2.59	3.32	5.37	0.56	6.85	5.94	1.29	5.00	3.97
Individual	–	0.46	0.16	1.87	1.39	–	2.17	–	0.52	1.99	0.19
Corporate	1.97	0.45	2.38	1.45	3.97	–	2.68	–	0.77	2.92	3.78
Social security contributions	–	–	–	0.45	0.13	–	–	–	–	0.02	–
Taxes on property	–	0.02	0.09	0.21	0.05	0.02	0.14	1.53	0.47	0.69	1.94
Taxes on goods and services	1.11	2.20	0.99	3.39	3.54	1.86	7.44	3.71	5.51	8.58	6.09
Taxes on international trade and transactions	0.87	1.75	0.27	1.15	3.12	1.95	6.06	0.46	3.40	4.57	5.61
Tax revenue	3.96	4.89	3.97	8.84	12.64	4.39	21.05	13.32	10.75	19.07	18.30

Notes:
Notice that taxes on income, profits and capital gains also include other unallocable taxes on income. Tax revenue also includes other taxes.
* First year available 1994.

Source: Our calculations from IMF *Government Finance Statistics Yearbook* (1999, 2000).

Table 4.1b Structure of tax revenue (percentage of GDP) in Asia in 2004

	China	India	Indonesia	Korea, Rep.	Malaysia*	Pakistan	Philippines	Singapore	Sri Lanka	Thailand	Vietnam
Tax on income, profits, capital gains	4.76	5.50	7.18	6.93	11.11	3.55	24.10	5.49	3.82	11.06	16.23
Individual	1.46	2.01	5.78	3.38	2.60	0.51	8.74	–	1.24	3.49	0.97
Corporate	3.30	3.49	1.40	3.56	8.50	2.90	11.36	–	1.54	7.57	15.26
Social security contributions	–	0.05	0.70	0.04	–	–	–	–	0.32	–	–
Taxes on property	0.23	0.01	0.88	0.43	0.05	0.01	0.06	1.12	–	0.01	1.02
Domestic taxes on goods and services	17.44	4.89	8.16	7.46	5.02	5.78	15.14	4.71	17.69	13.69	19.15
Taxes on international trade and transactions	–	2.14	0.77	0.98	1.31	1.91	10.65	0.01	4.49	2.81	5.95
Tax revenue	19.80	12.59	17.79	17.01	17.39	12.79	52.41	12.31	26.33	27.75	42.34

Notes:
Notice that taxes on income, profits and capital gains also include other unallocable taxes on income. Tax revenue also includes other taxes.
* Last year available 2003

Source: Our calculations from *IMF Government Finance Statistics Yearbook* (2006).

Firms enjoy a generous tax system, especially foreigner firms, which take advantage of a complex system of tax incentives, aimed at attracting foreign direct investments in specific sectors.[4] As a consequence, although tax incentives may generate a low level of taxation, corporate tax revenue is usually higher than personal income tax, with a large part of revenues coming from multinationals. Personal income tax is instead still quite embryonic in many countries (see Bernardi *et al.*, 2006).

Another very strong feature is that social contributions are very low. All countries have a very limited, approximately zero, pension system. This will be a crucial challenge for the economic and political development of Asian countries such as China, for example, which shows a rapid ageing of population.

These features reveal many policy issues for taxation and development in these countries: some of them apply more to a specific cluster of countries; some are general. Many studies have analysed and discussed them. Recently, Bernardi *et al.* (2006) have investigated the following policy issues suggesting directions for reforms: the improvement of tax administration and the control of tax evasion, the development of fiscal federalism, the assessment of incentives in corporate taxation, the introduction of a pension system, and the design of a personal income tax which would join a redistributive aim to mere efficiency goals. Fiscal decentralization is also crucial. Even India and China, giant countries, clearly difficult to administer only at the central level, have a low fiscal decentralization. Recent trends seem to move towards greater decentralization. Related to this, tax administration is another crucial area.

In this section, we argue that a relevant issue to be investigated is the development of democratic institutions. We show the role of the political regime on the current tax system and suggest the implications for the future. Before that, it is thus essential to provide an overview of data on the political regime of these countries.

To measure democracy, as we said in Chapter 3, we use different variables from the Polity IV dataset (2007) and Freedom House. In particular, Figures 4.2a and 4.2b show the values of the POLITY2 indicator in the period 1990–2004 for China, India, Indonesia, the Republic of Korea, Malaysia and Pakistan, and the Philippines, Singapore, Sri Lanka, Thailand and Vietnam respectively. Three results emerge: (i) China and Vietnam are characterized by the lowest absolute levels of the POLITY2 indicator (scoring −7

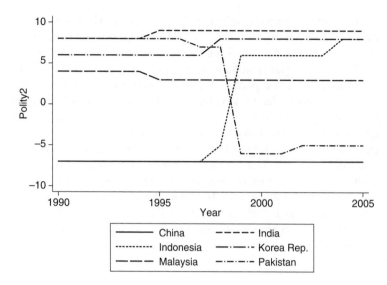

Source: Polity IV dataset (2007).

Figure 4.2a Democracy in Asia 1990–2004

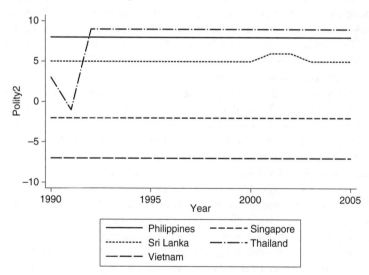

Source: Polity IV dataset (2007).

Figure 4.2b Democracy in Asia 1990–2004

throughout the period), followed by Singapore, which stays on a similar stable pattern of low values (−2 throughout the period); (ii) India, the Philippines, the Republic of Korea and, to a lesser extent, Sri Lanka and Malaysia have a tradition of high democracy; (iii) the other countries, especially the ones which entered the mid-1990s with low levels of democracy, that is Indonesia and Thailand, have experienced a certain variation of this indicator over time, mostly an ascendant path. Pakistan is the relevant exception, with the POLITY2 indicator falling at the end of the 1990s. Using the indicators from Freedom House we would reach similar results.

In the next section we empirically explore the relation between the evidence reported in Tables 4.1a and 4.1b and Figures 4.1a and 4.1b and that reported in Figures 4.2a and 4.2b, that is the link, if it exists, between political regimes and the level and structure of taxation.

Summary statistics of all variables are in Table 4.2.

4.3   POLITICAL REGIMES AND TAX REVENUE

We first run a pooled OLS regression for tax revenue and then several OLS regressions for the share of revenue coming from the six main taxes: personal income tax (PIT), corporate income tax (CIT), social security contributions (SS), goods and services taxes (GS), trade taxes (TRADE) and property taxes (PROP). Our set of independent variables includes different measures of the political regimes and fundamental economic variables. The political measures are: POLITY2 and its components DEMOC and AUTOC, FREEDOM1 and FREEDOM2, and the interaction between the regime durability and the POLITY2 indicator, DUR_POLITY. The fundamental economic variables are: the growth rate of real GDP per capita (GDPVAR),[5] the share of agriculture on GDP (AGR), the openness of the economy as a percentage of GDP (OPE) and the central government debt/GDP ratio (DEBT). Moreover, according to what we have called in Chapter 3 an 'enriched scenario', we add into the analysis some further control variables, to capture recent socio-economic trends in developing countries, which may also have an impact on the revenues collected and on redistributive policies. Specifically, these variables are: the share of population over 65 on total population (OLD), female labour force participation (FEMALE) as a percentage of female population between

Table 4.2 Summary statistics of all variables

Variable	Observations	Mean	Standard deviation	Minimum	Maximum
POLITY2	176	2.29	6.31	−7	9
DEMOC	176	4.76	3.53	0	9
AUTOC	176	2.47	2.85	0	7
DURABLE	176	26.70	18.36	0	57
FREEDOM1	175	4.40	1.39	2	7
FREEDOM2	176	4.17	1.90	1	7
TAX_REV	156	17.06	10.68	3.35	52.41
DIRECT	156	5.994	4.811	0.56	24.1
PIT	125	2.18	2.06	0.16	9.17
CIT	137	3.61	2.87	0.45	15.26
PROP	144	0.46	0.58	0.00	2.44
TRADE	153	2.89	2.83	0.01	12.35
GS	156	7.10	4.33	0.56	19.15
SS	53	0.38	0.38	0.02	1.63
GDPVAR	160	3.97	4.07	−9.44	15.22
OPE	152	77.83	46.99	15.70	228.90
DEBT	160	54.01	32.43	3.40	118.10
AGR	176	16.35	8.81	0.10	40.50
OLD	176	5.23	1.42	3.21	9.44
FEMALE	176	53.91	15.56	58.80	79.50
URBAN	176	45.07	24.75	15.10	100.00
DENSITY	176	700.47	1552.76	55.10	6191.29
SCHOOLING	34	64.82	19.54	26.20	97.17
SHADOW	77	28.86	13.10	9.80	54.30
GINI	29	40.02	5.94	30.10	49.20
CREDIT1	20	0.49	0.26	0.17	0.89
CREDIT2	20	0.62	0.38	0.18	1.25

15 and 64 years old, the percentage of urban population over the total population (URBAN), the number of people per square kilometre (DENSITY), the share of children of secondary school age who are currently enrolled in secondary school (SCHOOLING), the size of the shadow economy as a percentage of GDP (SHADOW), the Gini index (GINI), private credit by deposit money bank to GDP (CREDIT1) and private credit by deposit money bank and other financial instruments to GDP (CREDIT2). Finally, we run regressions without time fixed effects and then include them.

The results for tax revenue are in Tables 4.3a to 4.3g.

Table 4.3a shows that our basic specification, which includes only fundamental economic and political variables, explains tax revenue quite well (R^2 is between 0.28 and 0.47 and the F-test is in the standard interval). The different columns a) of the table refer to the different measures of political variables that we use in our analysis. They show that tax revenue is associated positively and significantly with POLITY2 and DEMOC and negatively with AUTOC and lower civil liberties (higher values of FREEDOM1) or political rights (higher values of FREEDOM2). Surprisingly, democratic regime durability has a negative relation with tax revenue. As for the economic fundamentals, the openness of the economy is significant in the specification with a positive sign; on the contrary, the growth rate of real GDP per capita and the central government debt/GDP ratio are not significantly related to tax revenue.[6] The share of agriculture over GDP appears significant and shows a positive sign only when combined with the political variable on the civil liberties measured by Freedom House and the one based on the interaction between the duration of the political regime and the POLITY2 indicator.

In Table 4.3b we enrich our basic specification by including a variable which captures one of the demographic changes under way in the region, that is the ageing process. The share of elderly in the population (OLD) turns out to be negatively related with tax revenue: more aged societies seem to be able to collect less tax revenue. However, the inclusion of this control variable does not change the sign and significance of the relation between tax revenue and political variables (POLITY2, DEMOC, AUTOC, FREEDOM1 and FREEDOM2).

A similar result is obtained when we control for the female labour force participation rate (Table 4.3c), to check for the possibility that higher tax revenue would depend on a greater female participation in employment. Though the female labour force participation is indeed positively related with tax revenue, our political variables remain significant.

In Chapter 3 we have argued that one of the main challenges for these countries is the growing need for a larger welfare state, owing, among other things, to urbanization. Thus, a higher percentage of urban population may potentially push to an increase of tax revenue to finance welfare expenditures. In Table 4.3d we check for the potential impact of the percentage of urban population on tax

Table 4.3a   Tax revenue and political regimes: fundamental economic and political variables

	(1a) TAX_REV	(1b) TAX_REV	(2a) TAX_REV	(2b) TAX_REV	(3a) TAX_REV	(3b) TAX_REV	(4a) TAX_REV	(4b) TAX_REV	(5a) TAX_REV	(5b) TAX_REV	(6a) TAX_REV	(6b) TAX_REV
CONS	11.971	8.12	7.666	3.61	16.763	13.511	19.26	15.892	18.82	15.291	6.022	1.319
	(3.05)**	(1.56)	(1.77)*	(0.67)	(4.57)***	(2.62)*	(5.3)***	(3.12)**	(5.21)***	(3.14)**	(1.46)	(0.27)
GDPVAR	−0.261	−0.218	−0.24	−0.199	−0.295	−0.252	−0.149	−0.116	−0.232	−0.217	−0.235	−0.015
	(−0.86)	(−0.69)	(−0.8)	(−0.64)	(−0.96)	(−0.8)	(−0.48)	(−0.36)	(−0.82)	(−0.74)	(−0.75)	(−0.05)
AGR	−0.188	0.094	−0.18	0.093	−0.202	0.09	0.13	0.404	−0.021	0.258	−0.074	0.37
	(−1.28)	(0.57)	(−1.23)	(0.58)	(−1.36)	(0.54)	(0.66)	(1.75)*	(−0.13)	(1.36)	(−0.46)	(2.11)*
OPE	0.084	0.097	0.09	0.104	0.078	0.089	0.111	0.125	0.098	0.112	0.088	0.107
	(3.07)**	(3.25)**	(3.35)**	(3.55)**	(2.77)**	(2.9)**	(3.85)***	(3.99)***	(3.64)***	(3.86)***	(3.48)**	(3.88)***
DEBT	0.015	−0.034	0.019	−0.027	0.011	−0.041	0.005	−0.037	0.004	−0.044	0.052	−0.006
	(0.56)	(−1.3)	(0.72)	(−1.06)	(0.42)	(−1.52)	(0.21)	(−1.33)	(0.13)	(−1.62)	(1.64)	(−0.2)
POLITY2	0.502	0.578									1.159	1.253
	(4.31)***	(4.83)***									(4.32)***	(4.87)***
DEMOC			0.944	1.052								
			(4.46)***	(4.85)***								
AUTOC					−1.018	−1.232						
					(−3.99)***	(−4.68)***						

Table 4.3a (continued)

	(1a) TAX_REV	(1b) TAX_REV	(2a) TAX_REV	(2b) TAX_REV	(3a) TAX_REV	(3b) TAX_REV	(4a) TAX_REV	(4b) TAX_REV	(5a) TAX_REV	(5b) TAX_REV	(6a) TAX_REV	(6b) TAX_REV
FREEDOM1							−3.082 (−3.85)***	−3.361 (−4.01)***				
FREEDOM2									−2.205 (−4.45)***	−2.362 (−4.82)***		
DURABLE											0.03 (0.68)	−0.033 (−0.77)
DUR_POLITY											−0.025 (−3.25)**	−0.027 (−3.42)**
TIME FIXED EFFECTS		YES (not signif.)		YES (not signif.)		YES (not signif.)		YES (not signif.)		YES (not signif.)		YES (not signif.)
No. of observations	126	126	126	126	126	126	126	126	126	126	126	126
Countries	11	11	11	11	11	11	11	11	11	11	11	11
R^2	0.30	0.39	0.31	0.40	0.28	0.38	0.33	0.41	0.35	0.43	0.35	0.47

Notes:
All variables are explained in Chapter 7. Robust t-statistics in parentheses.
* Significant at 10%; ** significant at 5%; *** significant at 1%.
Regressions b include time fixed effects.

Table 4.3b Tax revenue and political regimes: the impact of the percentage of people over 65 years old (OLD)

	(1a) TAX_REV	(1b) TAX_REV	(2a) TAX_REV	(2b) TAX_REV	(3a) TAX_REV	(3b) TAX_REV	(4a) TAX_REV	(4b) TAX_REV	(5a) TAX_REV	(5b) TAX_REV
CONS	20.16	26.515	16.414	22.513	24.336	31.195	23.655	27.69	25.732	31.254
	(2.93)**	(3.20)**	(2.5)*	(2.87)**	(3.32)**	(3.53)**	(3.33)**	(3.24)**	(3.49)**	(3.71)***
GDPVAR	−0.221	−0.036	−0.195	−0.007	−0.258	−0.08	−0.133	−0.026	−0.198	−0.065
	(−0.74)	(−0.12)	(−0.66)	(−0.02)	(−0.85)	(−0.26)	(−0.43)	(−0.08)	(−0.7)	(−0.23)
AGR	−0.336	−0.161	−0.336	−0.168	−0.343	−0.159	0.034	0.196	−0.153	0.024
	(−1.87)*	(−1.05)	(−1.89)*	(−1.11)	(−1.87)*	(−1.02)	(0.17)	(0.95)	(−0.83)	(0.14)
OPE	0.071	0.07	0.076	0.076	0.065	0.063	0.103	0.104	0.086	0.088
	(2.69)**	(2.49)*	(2.97)**	(2.79)**	(2.4)*	(2.16)*	(3.97)***	(3.79)***	(3.4)**	(3.31)**
DEBT	0.018	−0.035	0.023	−0.029	0.015	−0.042	0.008	−0.035	0.007	−0.044
	(0.67)	(−1.23)	(0.83)	(−1.02)	(0.54)	(−1.41)	(0.31)	(−1.22)	(0.25)	(−1.54)
OLD	−0.989	−2.166	−1.053	−2.233	−0.932	−2.092	−0.554	−1.44	−0.853	−1.899
	(−1.18)	(−2.27)*	(−1.25)	(−2.36)*	(−1.1)	(−2.16)*	(−0.73)	(−1.6)	(−1.08)	(−2.17)*
POLITY2	0.49	0.573								
	(4.34)***	(4.83)***								
DEMOC			0.93	1.057						
			(4.5)***	(4.89)***						
AUTOC					−0.976	−1.201				
					(−3.97)***	(−4.63)***				

Table 4.3b (continued)

	(1a) TAX_REV	(1b) TAX_REV	(2a) TAX_REV	(2b) TAX_REV	(3a) TAX_REV	(3b) TAX_REV	(4a) TAX_REV	(4b) TAX_REV	(5a) TAX_REV	(5b) TAX_REV
FREEDOM1							-2.979 (-4.06)***	-3.073 (-4)***		
FREEDOM2									-2.157 (-4.6)***	-2.28 (-4.95)***
TIME FIXED EFFECTS		YES (not signif.)		YES (not signif.)		YES (not signif.)		YES (not signif.)		YES (not signif.)
No. of observations	126	126	126	126	126	126	126	126	126	126
Countries	11	11	11	11	11	11	11	11	11	11
R^2	0.31	0.42	0.32	0.43	0.29	0.41	0.33	0.42	0.35	0.46

Notes:
All variables are explained in Chapter 7. Robust t-statistics in parentheses.
* Significant at 10%; ** significant at 5%; *** significant at 1%.
Regressions b include time fixed effects.

Table 4.3c   Tax revenue and political regimes: the impact of female labour force participation (FEMALE)

	(1a) TAX_REV	(1b) TAX_REV	(2a) TAX_REV	(2b) TAX_REV	(3a) TAX_REV	(3b) TAX_REV	(4a) TAX_REV	(4b) TAX_REV	(5a) TAX_REV	(5b) TAX_REV
CONS	-20.019	-23.126	-24.944	-27.741	-13.066	-16.435	-15.601	-23.185	-12.289	-16.304
	(-3.66)***	(-3.69)***	(-3.99)***	(-4.08)***	(-2.86)**	(-2.91)**	(-3.44)**	(-4.01)***	(-2.82)**	(-3.26)**
GDPVAR	-0.355	-0.385	-0.337	-0.369	-0.386	-0.417	-0.159	-0.188	-0.346	-0.419
	(-1.29)	(-1.31)	(-1.23)	(-1.26)	(-1.37)	(-1.41)	(-0.58)	(-0.73)	(-1.37)	(-1.59)
AGR	-0.124	0.056	-0.122	0.047	-0.132	0.063	0.483	0.67	0.121	0.278
	(-1.05)	(0.45)	(-1.04)	(0.38)	(-1.1)	(0.49)	(2.92)**	(3.76)***	(0.9)	(2.02)*
OPE	0.068	0.076	0.078	0.086	0.055	0.062	0.113	0.118	0.088	0.095
	(3.65)***	(3.69)***	(4.13)***	(4.17)***	(2.93)**	(2.97)**	(5.81)***	(6.2)***	(5.17)***	(5.14)***
DEBT	0.158	0.122	0.161	0.127	0.153	0.116	0.178	0.181	0.157	0.128
	(3.94)***	(3.43)**	(4.03)***	(3.57)**	(3.81)***	(3.23)**	(4.74)***	(5.29)***	(4.09)***	(3.77)***
FEMALE	0.475	0.46	0.458	0.44	0.491	0.481	0.604	0.667	0.519	0.513
	(6.58)***	(6.32)***	(6.44)***	(6.15)***	(6.71)***	(6.49)***	(7.41)***	(8.25)***	(6.85)***	(7.09)***
POLITY2	0.801	0.831								
	(6.08)***	(6.49)***								
DEMOC			1.393	1.428						
			(5.86)***	(6.29)***						
AUTOC					-1.815	-1.927				
					(-6.33)***	(-6.65)***				

65

Table 4.3c (continued)

	(1a) TAX_REV	(1b) TAX_REV	(2a) TAX_REV	(2b) TAX_REV	(3a) TAX_REV	(3b) TAX_REV	(4a) TAX_REV	(4b) TAX_REV	(5a) TAX_REV	(5b) TAX_REV
FREEDOM1							-5.649 (-6.7)***	-6.422 (-8.24)***		
FREEDOM2									-3.32 (-6.29)***	-3.388 (-6.9)***
TIME FIXED EFFECTS		YES (not signif.)		YES (not signif.)		YES (not signif.)		YES (not signif.)		YES (not signif.)
No. of observations	126	126	126	126	126	126	126	126	126	126
Countries	11	11	11	11	11	11	11	11	11	11
R^2	0.46	0.52	0.46	0.52	0.45	0.52	0.56	0.65	0.53	0.60

Notes:
All variables are explained in Chapter 7. Robust t-statistics in parentheses.
* Significant at 10%; ** significant at 5%; *** significant at 1%.
Regressions b include time fixed effects.

Table 4.3d   Tax revenue and political regimes: the impact of urbanization (URBAN)

	(1a) TAX_REV	(1b) TAX_REV	(2a) TAX_REV	(2b) TAX_REV	(3a) TAX_REV	(3b) TAX_REV	(4a) TAX_REV	(4b) TAX_REV	(5a) TAX_REV	(5b) TAX_REV
CONS	5.214	0.976	0.779	-3.755	9.829	6.378	15.815	12.366	13.517	9.661
	(0.7)	(0.11)	(0.1)	(-0.43)	(1.33)	(0.74)	(2.41)*	(1.51)	(2.1)*	(1.24)
GDPVAR	-0.228	-0.169	-0.203	-0.143	-0.265	-0.208	-0.144	-0.107	-0.21	-0.182
	(-0.76)	(-0.55)	(-0.69)	(-0.48)	(-0.87)	(-0.68)	(-0.47)	(-0.34)	(-0.74)	(-0.63)
AGR	-0.031	0.27	-0.014	0.281	-0.05	0.255	0.183	0.461	0.087	0.38
	(-0.15)	(1.05)	(-0.07)	(1.1)	(-0.23)	(0.99)	(0.78)	(1.64)	(0.39)	(1.45)
OPE	0.086	0.099	0.092	0.106	0.08	0.092	0.110	0.124	0.098	0.113
	(2.89)**	(3.05)**	(3.16)**	(3.33)**	(2.61)*	(2.72)**	(3.81)***	(3.94)***	(3.48)**	(3.67)***
DEBT	0.019	-0.031	0.022	-0.025	0.016	-0.037	0.008	-0.034	0.007	-0.041
	(0.67)	(-1.14)	(0.82)	(-0.92)	(0.55)	(-1.33)	(0.31)	(-1.25)	(0.25)	(-1.51)
URBAN	0.091	0.098	0.095	0.103	0.089	0.093	0.042	0.044	0.067	0.073
	(1.33)	(1.4)	(1.4)	(1.49)	(1.26)	(1.31)	(0.66)	(0.65)	(1.07)	(1.13)
POLITY2	0.471	0.546								
	(4.5)***	(4.95)***								
DEMOC			0.898	1.006						
			(4.68)***	(5)***						
AUTOC					-0.929	-1.145				
					(-4.03)***	(-4.69)***				

67

Table 4.3d (continued)

	(1a) TAX_REV	(1b) TAX_REV	(2a) TAX_REV	(2b) TAX_REV	(3a) TAX_REV	(3b) TAX_REV	(4a) TAX_REV	(4b) TAX_REV	(5a) TAX_REV	(5b) TAX_REV
FREEDOM1							-2.915 (-4.18)***	-3.179 (-4.14)***		
FREEDOM2									-2.1 (-4.82)***	-2.25 (-5.09)***
TIME FIXED EFFECTS		YES (not signif.)		YES (not signif.)		YES (not signif.)		YES (not signif.)		YES (not signif.)
No. of observations	126	126	126	126	126	126	126	126	126	126
Countries	11	11	11	11	11	11	11	11	11	11
R^2	0.31	0.40	0.32	0.41	0.30	0.39	0.33	0.41	0.35	0.44

Notes:
All variables are explained in Chapter 7. Robust t-statistics in parentheses.
* Significant at 10%; ** significant at 5%; *** significant at 1%.
Regressions b include time fixed effects.

Table 4.3e   Tax revenue and political regimes: the impact of population density (DENSITY)

	(1a) TAX_REV	(1b) TAX_REV	(2a) TAX_REV	(2b) TAX_REV	(3a) TAX_REV	(3b) TAX_REV	(4a) TAX_REV	(4b) TAX_REV	(5a) TAX_REV	(5b) TAX_REV
CONS	9.344	5.674	5.768	1.559	12.393	9.897	22.916	20.469	23.229	19.818
	(1.73)*	(0.77)	(1.05)	(0.22)	(2.16)**	(1.26)	(4.51)***	(2.62)**	(4.71)***	(2.75)***
GDPVAR	−0.278	−0.243	−0.253	−0.222	−0.316	−0.282	−0.117	−0.061	−0.21	−0.182
	(−0.9)	(−0.74)	(−0.83)	(−0.69)	(−1.01)	(−0.86)	(−0.36)	(−0.18)	(−0.73)	(−0.6)
AGR	−0.126	0.148	−0.127	0.146	−0.117	0.155	0.102	0.371	−0.083	0.196
	(−0.7)	(0.66)	(−0.71)	(0.66)	(−0.64)	(0.68)	(0.52)	(1.56)	(−0.46)	(0.91)
OPE	0.096	0.108	0.1	0.114	0.095	0.103	0.102	0.113	0.084	0.099
	(2.63)***	(2.63)***	(2.84)***	(2.88)***	(2.48)**	(2.40)**	(3.18)***	(3.09)***	(2.63)***	(2.72)***
DEBT	0.009	−0.039	0.014	−0.033	0.005	−0.046	0.01	−0.03	0.01	−0.037
	(0.32)	(−1.25)	(0.47)	(−1.05)	(0.17)	(−1.48)	(0.36)	(−0.95)	(0.33)	(−1.21)
DENSITY	0.006	0.005	0.005	0.005	0.008	0.006	−0.006	−0.007	−0.008	−0.007
	(0.76)	(0.62)	(0.67)	(0.62)	(0.99)	(0.73)	(−0.8)	(−0.85)	(−1.15)	(−0.96)
POLITY2	0.448	0.529								
	(3.71)***	(4.16)***								
DEMOC			0.866	0.974						
			(4.08)***	(4.34)***						
AUTOC					−0.839	−1.088				
					(−3.01)***	(−3.72)***				

Table 4.3e (continued)

	(1a) TAX_REV	(1b) TAX_REV	(2a) TAX_REV	(2b) TAX_REV	(3a) TAX_REV	(3b) TAX_REV	(4a) TAX_REV	(4b) TAX_REV	(5a) TAX_REV	(5b) TAX_REV
FREEDOM1							-3.451 (-3.70)***	-3.825 (-3.77)***		
FREEDOM2									-2.49 (-4.79)***	-2.642 (-4.87)***
TIME FIXED EFFECTS		YES (not signif.)		YES (not signif.)		YES (not signif.)		YES (not signif.)		YES (not signif.)
No. of observations	126	126	126	126	126	126	126	126	126	126
Countries	11	11	11	11	11	11	11	11	11	11
R^2	0.3	0.39	0.31	0.4	0.29	0.38	0.33	0.41	0.35	0.43

Notes:
All variables are explained in Chapter 7. Robust t-statistics in parentheses.
* Significant at 10%; ** significant at 5%; *** significant at 1%.
Regressions b include time fixed effects.
Singapore is out of the countries' sample because it is an outlier.

Table 4.3f   Tax revenue and political regimes: the impact of schooling enrolment (SCHOOLING)

	(1a) TAX_REV	(1b) TAX_REV	(2a) TAX_REV	(2b) TAX_REV
CONS	−34.176	−79.760	42.34	−12.925
	(−0.68)	(−0.96)	(1.68)	(−0.31)
GDPVAR	0.158	0.874	0.157	0.498
	(0.51)	(0.62)	(0.66)	(0.7)
AGR	3.067	7.168	1.253	5.5
	(1.85)*	(1.69)	(1.21)	(2.18)*
OPE	0.108	0.156	0.17	0.247
	(2.13)*	(01.52)	(5.03)***	(3.55)**
DEBT	−0.146	−0.87	0.074	−0.79
	(−0.68)	(−0.78)	(0.43)	(−1.25)
SCHOOLING	0.014	0.338	−0.285	−0.002
	(0.03)	(0.45)	(−1.33)	(−0.01)
POLITY2	3.419	3.967		
	(6.77)***	(3.82)**		
FREEDOM2			−10.963	−12.508
			(−12.58)***	(−10.39)***
TIME FIXED EFFECTS		YES (not signif.)		YES (not signif.)
No. of observations	21	21	21	21
Countries	11	11	11	11
R^2	0.80	0.85	0.91	0.94

Notes:
All variables are explained in Chapter 7. Robust t-statistics in parentheses.
* Significant at 10%; ** significant at 5%; *** significant at 1%.
Regressions b include time fixed effects.

revenue. Though the percentage of urban population is positively related to the level of tax revenue as a percentage of GDP, it is not significant in explaining it. More importantly, notice that the relationship between our political variables and the level of tax revenue is also robust to the inclusion of this control.

Similarly, in Table 4.3e we control for the density of the population[7] and, again, the relation between our political variables and the level of tax revenue holds its significance with the usual signs.

Education policies may also be related with tax revenue and

democracy (see Chapter 3). To control for the potential positive impact of schooling on tax revenue, in Table 4.3f we add to our basic specification a variable which measures secondary schooling enrolment. Unfortunately the number of observations is drastically reduced, and thus we have decided to report only the results with the POLITY2 and the FREEDOM2 indicators, which turn out to remain significantly and respectively positively and negatively related to tax revenue.

We then turn to the size of the shadow economy and we find a positive relationship with the level of tax revenue (Table 4.3g), when the ageing process and female labour market participation are also taken into account. However, our political measures are still significantly related with tax revenue and with the usual signs.

We finally control for the Gini index and the size of private credit. We however have few observations on these variables and thus we have decided not to show any table. Including the Gini index helps us to exclude that the relationship between democracy and tax revenue is driven only by the level of income inequality (see Chapter 3): the Gini index turns out to be positive and significant, but it does not alter the significance of the political variables. The credit market indicators (CREDIT1 and CREDIT2) are also useful controls since in developing countries a larger use of the credit market may represent a substitute for the absence of a sizeable pension scheme when social security contributions are small. Again, the relationship between tax revenue and our political variables is robust to the inclusion of these controls.

Tax revenue evolves over time in each country of our sample (see Figures 4.1a and 4.1b). Thus, in columns *b* of Tables 4.3a to 4.3g we add time fixed effects to explain the cross-country variation at the same year for each specification. We instead do not include country fixed effects since cross-country variation is exactly what we want to measure (see Kenny and Winer, 2006). Each country is considered only for 15 years, a too short time period to see sensible variation in the level of tax revenue and political indicators.

Interestingly, with time fixed effects, the political regime always remains significantly related to tax revenue with the same sign of the relationship.

Although we control for a number of potential sources of omitted variables bias, OLS estimates should not in principle be interpreted causally in a cross-sectional set-up. However, we would note that our main inference relates to the interaction between political variables

Table 4.3g *Tax revenue and political regimes: the impact of the shadow economy (SHADOW)*

	(1a) TAX_REV	(1b) TAX_REV	(2a) TAX_REV	(2b) TAX_REV	(3a) TAX_REV	(3b) TAX_REV	(4a) TAX_REV	(4b) TAX_REV	(5a) TAX_REV	(5b) TAX_REV
CONS	1.761	10.518	−0.425	7.92	4.545	14.066	3.815	12.148	5.901	16.122
	(0.24)	(1.16)	(−0.06)	(0.87)	(0.62)	(1.51)	(0.54)	(1.33)	(0.8)	(1.77)*
GDPVAR	−0.409	−0.106	−0.385	−0.082	−0.44	−0.141	−0.41	−0.165	−0.465	−0.231
	(−0.83)	(−0.25)	(−0.79)	(−0.19)	(−0.88)	(−0.32)	(−0.85)	(−0.41)	(−0.97)	(−0.54)
AGR	−0.695	−0.452	−0.703	−0.465	−0.689	−0.44	−0.388	−0.063	−0.56	−0.293
	(−2.65)*	(−2.2)*	(−2.68)*	(−2.24)*	(−2.61)*	(−2.19)*	(−1.83)*	(−0.3)	(−2.29)*	(−1.55)
OPE	−0.034	−0.027	−0.031	−0.022	−0.04	−0.034	−0.002	0.016	−0.015	−0.003
	(−1.44)	(−1.13)	(−1.33)	(−0.96)	(−1.53)	(−1.31)	(−0.09)	(0.7)	(−0.73)	(−0.13)
DEBT	0.137	0.09	0.14	0.093	0.133	0.086	0.153	0.126	0.138	0.093
	(1.9)*	(1.53)	(1.93)*	(1.56)	(1.85)*	(1.48)	(2.11)*	(2.03)*	(1.92)*	(1.57)
SHADOW	0.422	0.385	0.419	0.386	0.428	0.387	0.355	0.295	0.369	0.322
	(3.61)**	(3.27)**	(3.59)**	(3.34)**	(3.69)**	(3.25)**	(3.22)**	(2.61)**	(3.25)**	(2.72)**
OLD	−3.771	−4.65	−3.831	−4.707	−3.698	−4.566	−3.575	−4.204	−3.578	−4.309
	(−2.71)**	(−3.52)**	(−2.78)**	(−3.6)**	(−2.63)*	(−3.41)**	(−2.69)*	(−3.48)**	(−2.67)*	(−3.51)**
FEMALE	0.569	0.566	0.563	0.553	0.573	0.579	0.65	0.689	0.577	0.574
	(4.34)***	(4.59)***	(4.42)***	(4.65)***	(4.18)***	(4.45)***	(4.19)***	(4.87)***	(4.29)***	(4.67)***
POLITY2	0.384	0.524								
	(2.41)*	(3.13)**								

Table 4.3g (continued)

	(1a) TAX_REV	(1b) TAX_REV	(2a) TAX_REV	(2b) TAX_REV	(3a) TAX_REV	(3b) TAX_REV	(4a) TAX_REV	(4b) TAX_REV	(5a) TAX_REV	(5b) TAX_REV
DEMOC			0.697 (2.5)*	0.914 (3.2)**						
AUTOC					−0.815 (−2.12)*	−1.186 (−2.95)**				
FREEDOM1							−3.002 (−2.9)**	−4.061 (−4.23)***		
FREEDOM2									−1.587 (−2.82)**	−2.022 (−3.55)**
TIME FIXED EFFECTS		YES (not signif.)		YES (not signif.)		YES (not signif.)		YES (not signif.)		YES (not signif.)
No. of observations	57	57	57	57	57	57	57	57	57	57
Countries	11	11	11	11	11	11	11	11	11	11
R^2	0.63	0.72	0.63	0.72	0.62	0.71	0.65	0.75	0.64	0.73

Notes:
All variables are explained in Chapter 7. Robust t-statistics in parentheses.
* Significant at 10%; ** significant at 5%; *** significant at 1%.
Regressions b include time fixed effects.

(it does not matter how they are measured) and tax revenue. In this context, for example, the reverse causality of concern would refer to possible feedback effects of taxation on the political regime, probably a less compelling case. A similar argument would run for issues of omitted variable bias. Nonetheless, since our estimates are obtained on a fairly small sample and the magnitude of the estimated effects is small, there may be a concern about the presence of serious attenuation bias due to measurement error. Lacking credible instrumental variable strategy for this set-up, our use of different measures and different sources for the political regime (POLITY2, DEMOC, AUTOC, FREEDOM1 and FREEDOM2) represents a robustness check to our results.

4.4   POLITICAL REGIMES AND THE STRUCTURE OF TAXATION

Tables 4.4a to 4.4c show our results for the structure of taxation.

A first general result is that larger tax revenue is associated with a larger amount of each revenue source (with the exception of social security contributions and property taxes).[8] This result is in line with Kenny and Winer (2006): as the government gets larger, more taxes are obtained from almost each tax source. As total revenues grow, all bases are used more heavily.

A second interesting result is that the economic variables seem to be better associated with the structure and composition of tax revenue than with tax revenue itself. The growth rate of real GDP per capita is significantly associated with a higher level of trade and property taxes, and with a lower level of personal income taxes. Agriculture is negatively and significantly related with the tax base (with the exception of CIT and TRADE), meaning that countries where the share of agriculture is larger, typically more rural and less industrialized countries, have lower taxes. The urbanization trend will pose challenges towards an increase of taxation. Openness is associated with less personal, indirect and property taxation, and with more corporate taxation. Debt is coupled with a lower level of personal, trade and corporate taxes, and a higher level of property taxes and taxes on goods and services.

Coming back to the main purpose of our analysis, the political regime is also significantly related to the tax mix in the considered

Table 4.4a Structure of taxation and political regimes

	(1) PIT					(2) CIT				
CONS	1.065	0.86	1.349	1.873	1.54	-1.031	-0.845	-1.297	-1.226	-1.414
	(1.84)*	(1.42)	(2.25)*	(3.58)**	(2.67)**	(-2.11)*	(-1.71)*	(-2.6)*	(-2.55)*	(-2.85)**
GDPVAR	-0.059	-0.058	-0.06	-0.051	-0.06	-0.044	-0.043	-0.043	-0.041	-0.043
	(-1.63)	(-1.6)	(-1.66)*	(-1.52)	(-1.68)*	(-1.32)	(-1.32)	(-1.31)	(-1.18)	(-1.32)
AGR	-0.039	-0.038	-0.039	-0.016	-0.032	0.04	0.041	0.04	0.037	0.034
	(-1.76)*	(-1.74)*	(-1.78)*	(-0.67)	(-1.48)	(2.03)*	(2.04)*	(2.02)*	(1.61)	(1.62)
OPE	-0.032	-0.003	-0.004	0	-0.002	0.025	0.025	0.026	0.025	0.024
	(-1.64)	(-1.46)	(-1.83)*	(-0.1)	(-1.04)	(7.18)***	(7.09)***	(7.31)***	(6.63)***	(6.97)***
DEBT	-0.009	-0.009	-0.009	-0.008	-0.009	-0.008	-0.009	-0.008	-0.009	-0.008
	(-2.03)*	(-1.96)*	(-2.14)*	(-1.93)*	(-2.11)*	(-1.35)	(-1.4)	(-1.27)	(-1.35)	(-1.27)
TAX_REV	0.156	0.156	0.156	0.149	0.152	0.143	0.144	0.143	0.141	0.146
	(12.66)***	(12.69)***	(12.68)***	(13.28)***	(12.49)***	(10.12)***	(10.06)***	(10.18)***	(10.09)***	(10.34)***
POLITY2	0.028					-0.027				
	(1.54)					(-1.98)*				

	(1)	(2)	(3)	(4)	(5)	(6)	(7)	(8)
DEMOC	0.047 (1.5)							
AUTOC		−0.065 (−1.58)			−0.045 (−1.84)*			
FREEDOM1			−0.313 (−4.04)***			0.063 (2.1)*		
FREEDOM2				−0.132 (−2.4)*			0.057 (0.82)	0.107 (2.23)*
No. of observations	110	110	110	110	122	122	122	122
Countries	11	11	11	11	11	11	11	11
R²	0.81	0.81	0.83	0.82	0.77	0.77	0.77	0.78

Notes:
All variables are explained in Chapter 7. Robust t-statistics in parentheses.
* Significant at 10%; ** significant at 5%; *** significant at 1%.

Table 4.4b Structure of taxation and political regimes

	(3) SS					(4) GS				
CONS	0.888	0.885	0.814	0.865	0.933	4.674	5.217	3.73	2.894	3.397
	(2.66)*	(2.57)*	(2.39)*	(2.38)*	(2.68)*	(4.87)***	(4.71)***	(4.21)***	(3.49)**	(3.74)***
GDPVAR	0	−0.001	0.001	−0.001	−0.002	0.069	0.071	0.067	0.036	0.071
	(−0.02)	(−0.05)	(0.07)	(−0.06)	(−0.13)	(1)	(1.04)	(0.98)	(0.54)	(1.03)
AGR	−0.034	−0.033	−0.036	−0.035	−0.028	−0.167	−0.165	−0.168	−0.245	−0.19
	(−1.73)*	(−1.66)	(−1.86)*	(−1.77)*	(−1.34)	(−4.54)***	(−4.47)***	(−4.61)***	(−5.55)***	(−4.89)***
OPE	−0.002	−0.002	−0.002	−0.002	−0.002	−0.018	−0.019	−0.016	−0.025	−0.021
	(−2.49)*	(−2.3)*	(−2.63)*	(−2.28)*	(−2.03)*	(−3.86)***	(−3.81)***	(−3.75)***	(−4.79)***	(−4.01)***
DEBT	0.003	0.003	0.003	0.003	0.002	0.021	0.02	0.023	0.024	0.022
	(1.3)	(1.24)	(1.42)	(1.14)	(0.93)	(1.95)*	(1.84)*	(2.11)*	(2.24)*	(2.04)*
TAX_REV	0.003	0.002	0.006	0.002	−0.002	0.337	0.337	0.337	0.351	0.346
	(0.44)	(0.24)	(0.76)	(0.31)	(−0.23)	(13.7)***	(13.63)***	(13.81)***	(14.32)***	(13.4)***
POLITY2	−0.004					−0.089				
	(−0.45)					(−2.04)*				

	(1)	(2)	(3)	(4)	(5)	(6)	(7)	(8)
DEMOC	-0.001 (-0.09)				-0.137 (-1.84)*			
AUTOC		0.021 (0.98)				0.231 (2.27)*		
FREEDOM1			0.011 (0.19)				0.742 (3.44)**	
FREEDOM2				-0.024 (-0.86)				0.355 (2.27)*
No. of observations	50	50	50	50	126	126	126	126
Countries	11	11	11	11	11	11	11	11
R^2	0.15	0.15	0.15	0.15	0.71	0.71	0.73	0.71

Notes:
All variables are explained in Chapter 7. Robust t-statistics in parentheses.
* Significant at 10%; ** significant at 5%; *** significant at 1%.

Table 4.4c Structure of taxation and political regimes

	(5) TRADE					(6) PROP				
CONS	-4.249	-4.594	-3.682	-3.645	-3.63	0.663	0.629	0.724	0.604	0.713
	(-11.29)***	(-11.86)***	(-9.82)***	(-9.56)***	(-9.43)***	(7.43)***	(6.71)***	(7.46)***	(6.3)***	(6.98)***
GDPVAR	0.049	0.048	0.049	0.05	0.043	0.012	0.012	0.011	0.01	0.011
	(1.98)*	(1.92)*	(2.03)*	(1.94)*	(1.72)*	(2.14)*	(2.14)*	(2.14)*	(1.7)*	(2.03)*
AGR	0.178	0.177	0.179	0.195	0.186	-0.032	-0.032	-0.032	-0.034	-0.031
	(9.56)***	(9.57)***	(9.53)***	(8.92)***	(9.82)***	(-7.93)***	(-7.89)***	(-7.99)***	(-7.8)***	(-7.84)***
OPE	0.002	0.003	0.001	0.004	0.004	-0.002	-0.002	-0.002	-0.003	-0.002
	(1.27)	(1.55)	(0.76)	(1.86)*	(1.86)*	(-5.1)***	(-4.86)***	(-5.35)***	(-4.88)***	(-4.57)***
DEBT	-0.009	-0.008	-0.01	-0.008	-0.009	0.005	0.005	0.005	0.005	0.005
	(-2.2)*	(-2.01)*	(-2.46)*	(-2.06)*	(-2.13)*	(4.03)***	(4.02)***	(4.02)***	(3.79)***	(3.94)***
TAX_REV	0.239	0.24	0.24	0.241	0.238	-0.001	-0.001	-0.001	0.001	-0.001
	(19.77)***	(19.49)***	(20.12)***	(18.95)***	(19.44)***	(-0.82)	(-0.78)	(-0.84)	(0.3)	(-0.71)
POLITY2	0.055					0.006				
	(5.25)***					(1.47)				

	(1)	(2)	(3)	(4)	(5)	(6)	(7)	(8)
DEMOC	0.087 (4.68)***				0.009 (1.24)			
AUTOC		−0.14 (−5.57)***				−0.014 (−1.72)*		
FREEDOM1			−0.207 (−2.74)**				0.031 (1.32)	
FREEDOM2				−0.158 (−3.91)***				−0.012 (−0.86)
No. of observations	123	123	123	123	115	115	115	115
Countries	11	11	11	11	11	11	11	11
R^2	0.88	0.89	0.88	0.88	0.29	0.29	0.29	0.28

Notes:
All variables are explained in Chapter 7. Robust t-statistics in parentheses.
* Significant at 10%; ** significant at 5%; *** significant at 1%.

countries. More democracy, measured by civil liberties and political rights and by the Polity IV dataset indicators respectively, induces more personal income taxation and less corporate income taxation. These results are also underlined by Kenny and Winer (2006), but are not completely confirmed by their empirical analysis. Turning to indirect taxes, democracies are associated with smaller goods and services taxes than autocracies. Notice also that according to our results more democracy is coupled with larger trade taxes. As regards property taxes, we only find that their level reduces when we consider the autocratic regime, while surprisingly there is no significant effect of the political variables on social security contributions.[9] This raises some doubt about the possibility that there could be a relation between the political regime and the size of pensions (as in Mulligan *et al.*, 2004).

NOTES

1. The main government expenditures were for general public services (public debt transactions and general transfers between levels of government) and economic affairs (agriculture, forestry, fishing and hunting, transport, fuel and energy).
2. This interval of time is justified by the data availability. Notice that it is an interesting period, since the selected countries show some variability both in their political regimes and in their tax levels and structure.
3. Using data from the IMF *Government Finance Statistics Yearbook*, 2004 is the last year available.
4. These countries (with exception of the Republic of Korea) are not forced to respect the OECD rules against harmful tax competition. Many experts have advocated the introduction of a world tax organization to avoid the anti-competitive outcomes of the tax holiday regimes, especially in China (Tanzi, 1999).
5. We do not include directly real GDP per worker to avoid the risk of endogeneity given that the dependent variables are expressed as a percentage of GDP. Also Kenny and Winer (2006) use the coefficient variation in real GDP as an explanatory variable which may capture the impact of a change in GDP on taxation.
6. As regards the central government debt/GDP, the presence of time fixed effects changes the sign of the relation with tax revenue.
7. We have excluded Singapore, because this is an outlier with respect to population density.
8. The presence of tax revenue among the explanatory variables may produce endogeneity problems. We have run the regressions omitting this variable and the results on the determinants of the tax mix remain very similar. Including tax revenue may however be important in a context with different political regimes, because it shows that the level of each source of tax revenue follows the level of total revenue and there are no compensations of one source with another.
9. Notice that, as done before, we also try to consider as an explanatory variable the regime durability. However, we find only a negative and significant relation of this variable with the level of CIT and a positive and significant relation with the share of property taxes. All other relations are not significant.

APPENDIX TO CHAPTER 4: HISTORICAL NOTES

China

After the Chinese Civil War between the Nationalists and the Communists, the People's Republic of China began to administer mainland China. It was established in 1949, with the Communist Party of China (CCP) led by Mao Zedong giving rise to a democratic dictatorship. From the late 1970s, the Republic of China started to implement a democratic multi-party state in Taiwan and the surrounding islands, the territories still under its control. Both states claimed to be the sole legitimate ruler of all of China, but, at the international level, the People's Republic of China forced a refusal to officially recognize the Republic of China and so maintained most of the official diplomatic relations.

India

In India, the Indian National Congress (INC) led the federal government for most of the years after its independence, enjoying a parliamentary majority until the 1990s with only the exception of two short periods during the 1970s and late 1980s. From 1996 to 1998 there was a period of political instability which ended with the creation of the National Democratic Alliance by the Bharatiya Janata Party (BJP) and smaller regional parties, the first non-INC and coalition government to complete a full five-year term. In 2004 elections the INC again won the largest number of seats and formed a coalition government supported by left wing parties and members opposed to the BJP.

Indonesia

In Indonesia, General Suharto came to power in 1966. During his government, the authoritarian New Order, he severely restricted civil liberties and promoted electoral rules by which he was able to split the power between his own Golkar Party and the military. In 1996, the Indonesian Democratic Party (PDI) stopped supporting the regime and started to assert its independence thanks to the new leader Megawati Sukarnoputri. Many democracy forums were organized, but several Megawati supporters were killed and arrested.

In 1997 and 1998 the Asian financial crisis increased popular discontent with the New Order and led to riots that forced Suharto to
resign. During the *Reformasi* era that followed Suharto's resignation, Indonesian political and governmental structures underwent
major reforms leading to a strengthening of democratic processes,
including a regional autonomy programme, and the first direct presidential election in 2004.

Malaysia

Since its independence in 1957, Malaysia has been governed by a
multi-racial coalition composed of 14 parties, the Barisan Nasional,
whose prominent members are the United Malays National
Organization (UMNO), the Malaysian Chinese Association (MCA)
and the Malaysian Indian Congress (MIC). There is a general agreement on the fact that, although authoritarianism in the country
preceded the administration of the fourth prime minister, Mahathir
bin Mohamad, he carried the process forward substantially from
1981 to 2003 with his criticisms of Western and developed countries.
In the 2004 general election, with Mahathir's successor, Dato' Seri
Abdullah Ahmad Badawi, the current prime minister, the Barisan
Nasional got to control 92 per cent of the seats in Parliament. In
recent years the opposition, which has little access to the media, cam-
paigned for free, clean and fairer elections. A setback for the ruling
party happened in 2008 and was determined especially by rising
inflation, crime and ethnic tensions.

Pakistan

Pakistan changed democratic for non-democratic institutions in
the late 1990s, but restored democracy in 2007. Military presidents
were in power from 1958 to 1971 and from 1977 to 1988 when
Benazir Bhutto was elected prime minister. Her government was
followed by that of Nawaz Sharif, and the two leaders alternated
until the military coup by General Pervez Musharraf in 1999, who
became President in 2001. General elections were held in 2002 and
Musharraf transferred executive powers to the newly elected prime
minister, Zafarullah Khan Jamali, who was succeeded in the 2004
prime-ministerial election by Shaukat Aziz. Although there were
a number of failures in its tenure, the government of 2002 was the

first elected government in Pakistan's history to complete its full five years. In 2007 new elections were called, but the assassination of Benazir Bhutto during the election campaign led to a postponement of the elections and nationwide riots. Bhutto's Pakistan People's Party (PPP) won the highest number of seats in the elections held in February 2008, and in August Musharraf resigned from the presidency when faced with impeachment.

Philippines

Since its independence in 1946, a period of political instability and communist and Muslim insurgencies characterized the Philippines, especially when Ferdinand Marcos was in power as elected president declaring martial law. The winner of the election of 1986, Corazon C. Aquino, the widow of the assassinated opposition leader Benigno Aquino Jr., took over the government and called for the need to think about a new constitution after the People Power Revolution led by liberal parties. Although national debt and corruption together with communist and Islamic separatist movements slackened the process, the introduction of democracy and the implementation of government reforms succeeded.

The Republic of Korea

After the division, the history of South Korea was characterized by alternating periods of democratic and autocratic rule. The First Republic, formally established in 1948, was associated with a democratic government at least until the Korean War in 1950. Then it became increasingly autocratic. In 1960, following the April revolution, the First Republic collapsed and in a new parliamentary election the Democratic Party came to power. The Second Republic was established. However, in less than a year this democratic government was replaced by an autocratic military regime. Major-General Park Chung-hee won the election of 1963 and stayed in power during the Third and Fourth Republics, declaring martial law and establishing a new constitution that gave him effective control over the parliament, although the Korean economy developed significantly during his tenure. After Park's murder in 1979, the Fifth Republic began. This period showed extensive efforts of reform and laid the foundations for the quite stable democratic system of the Sixth Republic started in 1987 with democratic elections that led to a successful and well-functioning liberal and modern democracy.

Singapore

In Singapore, a hybrid regime, in which one can find democratic and authoritarian features, and a one-party state, the People's Action Party (PAP) has controlled the political process since 1959 by threatening the electorate to influence their votes and using censorship and gerrymandering against the opposition to discourage and hamper its success. The prime minister Lee Kuan Yew, elected in 1959, was replaced in 1990 by Goh Chok Tong and in 2004 by his son Lee Hsien Loong. Since 1966, when it became the sole representative party, the PAP has always had a majority in the parliament, and from 1988 to 2006 it was returned to power on nomination day thanks to no candidates being fielded by the opposition parties.

Sri Lanka

Sri Lanka can be considered a multi-party democracy. The main rival coalitions are the left-wing Sri Lanka Freedom Party (SLFP) and the right-wing United National Party (UNP), this latter in power during the period 1977–93. Since the 1980s, the army has led the government opposition to the militants of the Marxist Janatha Vimukthi Peramuna (JVP) and of the Liberation Tigers of Tamil Eelam (LTTE), a terrorist organization that fights for the creation of an independent state in the north and the east of the island. This on-and-off civil war between the government and the LTTE caused significant damage to the politics, population, environment and economy of the country. In 2002 a ceasefire agreement was signed with international mediation, but unfortunately in late 2005 the hostilities started again, leading to a violation of international humanitarian law and to the formal withdrawal by the government from the ceasefire agreement in 2008.

Thailand

After decades of political instability during which military regimes or elite politicians replaced each other, Thailand eventually progressed towards a stable prosperity and democracy in the 1980s. Democratic political institutions slowly gained greater authority and in 1988 the leader of the Chart Thai Party (Thai Nation Party) Chatichai Choonhavan came to power as the first democratically elected prime minister. However, three years later, a *coup d'état* ended his term. Following the country's massive request concerning the reintroduction of democratic rule, the army commander Suchinda Kraprayoon resigned as prime minister and, after the interim government of Anand Panyarachun, in the election of 1992 the political parties that had opposed the military won by a narrow majority. In 1997 the People's Constitution was promulgated: many human rights were explicitly acknowledged, and measures were established to ensure the stability of elected governments. From 2001 to 2006 Thailand experimented with the tenure of Thaksin Shinawatra and his Thai Rak Thai (TRT) party. Following corruption scandals, in 2005 there were public protests by the People's Alliance for Democracy against Thaksin's regime and widespread requests for his resignation and impeachment. A period of political turmoil started. In 2006 a new *coup d'état* led to the abrogation of the 1997 Constitution, the promulgation of a new one and new elections in 2007.

Vietnam

In the politics of Vietnam, the central role of the Communist Party was reaffirmed by the new state constitution of 1992 that at the same time identified in the National Assembly the people's most representative institution with legislative powers. However, only in recent years has the authority of this body become more effective even if still subject to Communist Party direction. The executive organization of the party, the Politburo, consists of 14 members holding high positions in the government, the National Assembly and the Central Military Commission, which determines military policy. There are no legally recognized opposition parties.

5. Latin America

5.1 INTRODUCTION

This chapter focuses on a sample of Latin American countries, which includes Argentina, Bolivia, Brazil, Chile, Colombia, Costa Rica, the Dominican Republic, Ecuador, El Salvador, Guatemala, Haiti, Honduras, Mexico, Nicaragua, Panama, Paraguay, Peru, Uruguay and Venezuela.[1]

Latin America is a crucial area to investigate when one analyses the relationship between taxation and political regimes. As we will see, this relationship differentiates Latin America from other areas of the world, and thus justifies why a specific analysis focused only on Latin American countries is interesting and recommended.

Most Latin American countries have only recently experienced a transition towards democracy. With the exception of 'old' democracies such as Costa Rica or Colombia, while in the 1950s only a minority of Latin American countries could be considered democracies, in the 1990s a large majority of them accomplished the transition to a democratic political organization, which has generally represented the defeat of the armed forces' political power, although with several specific features. More detailed historical information on the political regimes characterizing our sample of Latin American countries are reported in the appendix to this chapter.

As analysed in Chapter 2, the literature underlines that the level of democratization may have relevant implications for economics. Some of the predictions of this literature however are to a certain extent at odds with what we observe in the Latin American context. In general, the economic performances of Latin American countries have been rather poor and disappointing, in particular in the years before and right after democratization: on average the lowest growth rates were in the 1980s, that is during the transition period. This poor economic performance is difficult to explain according to the 'modernization' theories. Focusing in particular on taxation, although we find a positive association between the level of democratization and the total level of tax revenue, there is no systematic relation between democracy and direct taxes, nor is there evidence of a rebalancing of tax composition in favour of more labour and less consumption taxation. These facts cannot be explained if we represent the functioning of a democracy through a standard median voter model, which aggregates voters' preferences: in this area, among the most unequal regions in the world (see Gómez Sabaini and Martner, 2008; Barreix *et al.*, 2006), the popular demand for redistribution turns out to be very high. Since indirect taxes may be regressive, the preference for redistribution should translate into more direct taxes.[2] We would thus expect significant increases mainly of personal income taxation with higher scores of democracy. This does not seem to happen in this area of the world.

In this chapter we first assess the evidence using our dataset and then we make an effort to provide possible explanations of this 'puzzling' non-relationship (or even inverse relationship) between direct taxes and democratic political regimes. Following Rodriguez (2001), many political factors have to be included to account for Latin America's overall poor economic outcomes: political instability, inequality in the distribution of political and economic power, corruption and rent-seeking, or vested interests. We will try to classify in two groups the specific elements which may have played a role in keeping personal income taxes low despite the democratic transition: (i) the quality of democracy, with a low level of representation and a relevant weight of lobby, elites and interest groups, and (ii) the development of financial institutions. We should also remember that international organizations, such as the IMF and the World Bank, have played a crucial role in the design of fiscal systems and fiscal reforms in many Latin American countries. The tax systems in place thus strongly reflect the plans of these external organizations, which are not necessarily in line with the preferences of their democratic societies.

5.2 OVERVIEW OF TAX SYSTEMS AND POLITICAL REGIMES

Figures 5.1a, 5.1b and 5.1c show the evolution of tax revenue as a percentage of GDP for our sample of Latin American countries in the period 1990–2004. Tax revenue as a percentage of GDP is

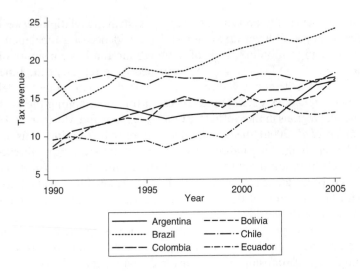

Source: CEPAL (2008), http://websie.eclac.cl/sisgen/ConsultaIntegrada.asp

Figure 5.1a   The evolution of tax revenue (percentage of GDP) in Latin America 1990–2004

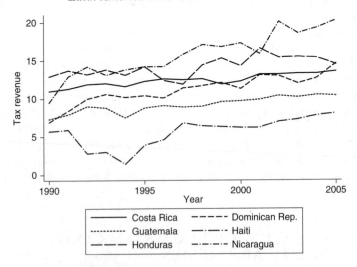

Source: CEPAL (2008), http://websie.eclac.cl/sisgen/ConsultaIntegrada.asp

Figure 5.1b   The evolution of tax revenue (percentage of GDP) in Latin America 1990–2004

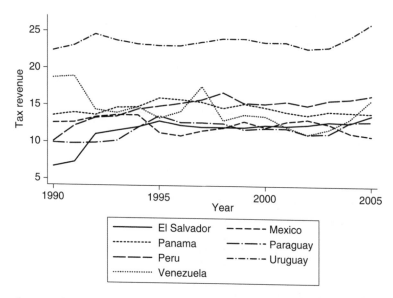

Source: CEPAL (2008), http://websie.eclac.cl/sisgen/ConsultaIntegrada.asp

Figure 5.1c The evolution of tax revenue (percentage of GDP) in Latin America 1990–2004

typically low in this area, everywhere lower than 20 per cent (with the exception of Brazil, where it rose above 20 per cent in the late 1990s, though it remained lower than 25 per cent) and for some countries well below 10 per cent. The average value for the entire Latin America area in 2004 was 16.6 per cent (CEPAL (2008), http://websie.eclac.cl/sisgen/ConsultaIntegrada.asp), compared with an EU25 average of 39.3 per cent (Eurostat, 2007, see Data Appendix in Chapter 7).

All countries show a relatively flat pattern, in particular Argentina, Chile, Uruguay and Paraguay. Colombia is the only country which experienced a quite ascendant path of tax revenue/GDP in the period 1990–2004 (the democratic transition here happened much earlier, in 1957).

If we turn our attention to political regimes, as illustrated by Figures 5.2a–5.2d, the variation of democracy over the years is more substantial. The figures make clear when the democratic transition happened in these countries in the considered period (see the appendix to this chapter for more detailed historical information).

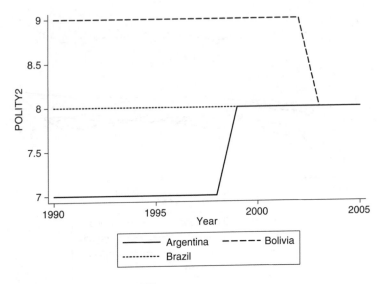

Source: Polity IV dataset (2007).

Figure 5.2a Democracy in Latin America 1990–2004

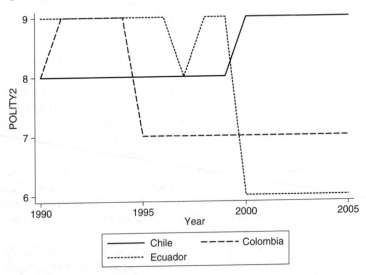

Source: Polity IV dataset (2007).

Figure 5.2b Democracy in Latin America 1990–2004

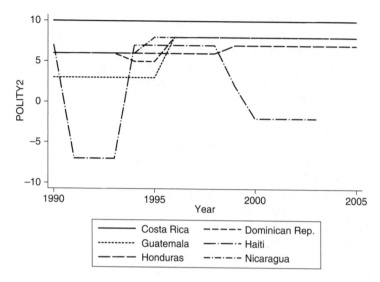

Source: Polity IV dataset (2007).

Figure 5.2c Democracy in Latin America 1990–2004

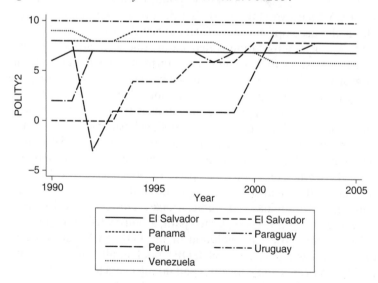

Source: Polity IV dataset (2007).

Figure 5.2d Democracy in Latin America 1990–2004

Despite the specific features that gave birth to the democratization process in each country, a common element of the successive development and, to a certain extent, of the current status
of democracy in Latin America relies on its implications for the
economy. Latin American citizens seem to support democratic
regimes mainly because they are convinced that these are beneficial for their economies. Seventy-two per cent of Latin Americans
believe that democracy is the only political system which can contribute to economic development (Latinobarometro polls 2004 in
Santiso, 2006). Interestingly, this value increases to 84 per cent in
Uruguay and 79 per cent in Argentina, the countries which have
experienced the most dramatic shocks and financial crises in the
area. In other words, as noticed by Santiso (2006), it seems that
Latin American citizens are becoming 'politically mature'. They
can distinguish between democracy as a political system, which they
consider the best environment for growth (on average, according to
the poll on human values 1995–2000, again in Santiso, 2006, more
than 80 per cent of Latin Americans approve of democratic ideals),
and the actual economic outcomes reached by the functioning of
their democratic governments and political leaders, which may fail
to satisfy their expectations. In fact the average rate of satisfaction
about the accomplishments of democracy does not exceed 62 per
cent. A crucial implication is that Latin American citizens are particularly sensitive to the economic performances (especially in terms
of growth and inflation) accomplished by their leaders, and they are
ready to punish those leaders who do not achieve the expected economic goals. At the same time, this implies that economic reforms
are a main platform proposed by political parties to gain votes.
This is especially true in the context of taxation, where reforms may
represent a politically feasible and optimal strategy to gain support,
since there still exists potential space for both increasing the fiscal
pressure and rebalancing the composition of the tax revenue, currently mainly dominated by indirect taxes. However, fiscal policies
do not really follow this suggested path, as illustrated by Figure 5.3.

Figure 5.3 shows the evolution of the POLITY2 indicator and
direct taxes as a percentage of GDP,[3] pooling all countries of our
Latin American sample together and taking average values for each
year. Notice that, while the political variable shows a minimum at
the beginning of the 1990s and then has an ascendant path, in particular up to 1996, direct taxes are almost stable (and low) until the

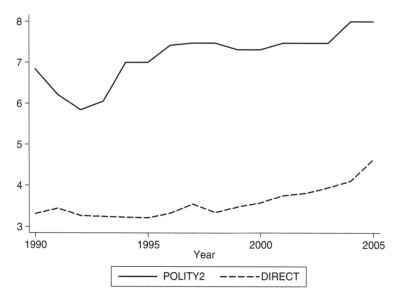

Source: Polity IV dataset (2007); CEPAL (2008), http://websie.eclac.cl/sisgen/ConsultaIntegrada.asp

Figure 5.3   The evolution of democracy and direct taxes in Latin America 1990–2004

late 1990s and then show a limited (less than 1 per cent) increase. Between 1992 and 1996 the POLITY2 indicator rises substantially, while direct taxes are almost stable. This evidence may suggest that there exists some delay in the response of taxation to democratization, or that the fiscal variable is not as responsive to the political regime as predicted by standard theories.

To better investigate this relationship between direct taxes and the political regime, in Figure 5.4 we plot the POLITY2 indicator and the level of direct taxes for the considered period for a selection of countries. The figure shows a quite surprising result: the patterns of the indicator POLITY2 and the level of direct taxes are diverging over time. In other words, the selected countries show clearly that when a country becomes more democratic this is not necessarily associated with an increase in direct taxes. Direct taxes stay stable at quite low levels (see in particular the case of Mexico).

There are also countries such as Bolivia, Colombia and Ecuador

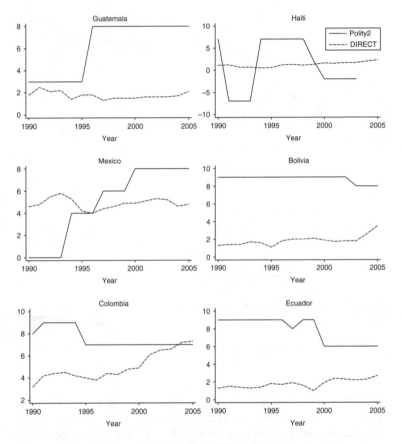

Source: Polity IV dataset (2007); CEPAL (2008), http://websie.eclac.cl/sisgen/
ConsultaIntegrada.asp

Figure 5.4   *The evolution of democracy and direct taxes for some
Latin American countries 1990–2004*

that have experienced a reduction of the POLITY2 indicator in the
considered period, with a slight increase in direct taxes (see Colombia
in particular), suggesting even a reverse relationship. We will further
investigate this evidence later on in this chapter.

Tables 5.1a and 5.1b provide an overview of tax revenue and its
structure as a percentage of GDP in 1990 and in 2004. A typical
feature of Latin American tax systems is that they are continuously

Table 5.1a Structure of tax revenue (percentage of GDP) in Latin America in 1990 (central government)

	Direct taxes	Individual	Corporate	Taxes on property	Social security contributions	Indirect taxes	Taxes on international trade and transactions	Tax revenue
Argentina	1.5	–	–	1.0	4.1	6.5	1.6	12.1
Bolivia	1.3	0.4	0.4	0.0	1.2	6.0	1.3	8.4
Brazil	7.2	0.3	1.4	1.2	8.1	2.6	0.4	17.9
Chile	2.9	0.7	1.7	0.5	1.6	10.9	2.3	15.4
Colombia	3.2	–	–	0.0	0.8	4.6	1.3	8.7
Costa Rica	2.2	–	–	0.4	0.2	8.6	3.1	11.0
Dominican Rep	2.4	0.0	0.0	0.2	0.1	4.5	2.1	6.9
Ecuador	1.3	–	–	0.0	2.3	6.1	2.4	9.6
El Salvador	2.5	0.7	1.1	0.5	1.4	2.8	1.3	6.7
Guatemala	1.8	0.0	0.0	0.2	–	5.5	1.7	7.3
Haiti	1.1	0.6	0.6	0.0	–	4.6	1.4	5.7

Table 5.1a (continued)

	Direct taxes	Individual	Corporate	Taxes on property	Social security contributions	Indirect taxes	Taxes on international trade and transactions	Tax revenue
Honduras	3.0	0.8	0.7	0.1	0.6	9.3	4.7	12.9
Mexico	4.6	1.9	2.5	0.1	1.9	6.1	0.9	12.6
Nicaragua	2.3	–	–	0.4	0.9	6.3	1.3	9.5
Panama	4.3	0.2	1.2	0.6	4.5	4.9	2.3	13.6
Paraguay	1.5	–	1.2	0.3	0.5	7.9	2.3	9.9
Peru	1.8	0.1	0.6	1.2	0.9	7.3	1.2	10.1
Uruguay	2.3	–	1.1	1.3	7.8	12.3	2.0	22.4
Venezuela	15.7	0.0	14.3	0.1	0.9	2.1	1.4	18.7

Notes: Notice that direct taxes include personal and corporate income tax, taxes on property and other direct taxes. Indirect taxes include taxes on goods and services, taxes on international trade and transactions and other indirect taxes.

Source: CEPAL (2008), http://websie.eclac.cl/sisgen/ConsultaIntegrada.asp; Bernardi *et al.* (2008).

Table 5.1b Structure of tax revenue (percentage of GDP) in Latin America in 2004 (central government)

	Direct taxes	Individual	Corporate	Taxes on property	Social security contributions	Indirect taxes	Taxes on international trade, and transactions	Tax revenue
Argentina	5.1	1.4	3.4	1.6	3.0	8.4	2.7	16.6
Bolivia	2.6	0.2	0.0	0.5	1.9	10.7	1.0	15.2
Brazil	9.3	0.3	1.9	1.6	12.1	1.6	0.5	23.1
Chile	5.2	1.1	2.9	0.7	1.4	10.4	0.4	17.0
Colombia	7.2	–	–	1.3	2.8	7.2	0.9	17.3
Costa Rica	3.8	–	–	0.5	0.3	9.2	1.1	13.3
Dominican Rep	2.9	0.7	1.3	0.2	0.0	9.8	4.1	12.7
Ecuador	2.3	–	–	0.2	3.1	7.3	1.4	12.7
El Salvador	3.5	–	–	0.1	1.7	7.6	1.1	12.8
Guatemala	1.7	0.0	0.0	0.0	0.2	8.6	1.4	10.5
Haiti	2.0	0.9	1.1	0.0	–	5.9	2.5	7.8

Table 5.1b (continued)

	Direct taxes	Individual	Corporate	Taxes on property	Social security contributions	Indirect taxes	Taxes on international trade and transactions	Tax revenue
Honduras	3.9	0.9	0.8	0.2	1.0	10.6	1.1	15.4
Mexico	4.6	–	–	0.2	1.5	5.3	0.4	11.4
Nicaragua	4.5	–	–	0.0	3.5	11.3	1.0	19.3
Panama	4.0	0.2	1.2	0.4	5.6	4.6	2.3	14.2
Paraguay	2.1	–	2.1	0.0	1.1	9.8	2.2	12.9
Peru	4.3	1.2	2.2	0.3	1.6	10.1	1.2	16.0
Uruguay	4.3	–	2.5	1.8	5.7	14.3	1.4	24.4
Venezuela	4.8	0.0	1.8	1.0	0.6	7.8	1.0	13.3

Note: Notice that direct taxes include personal and corporate tax, taxes on property and other direct taxes. Indirect taxes include taxes on goods and services, taxes on international trade and transactions and other indirect taxes.

Source: CEPAL (2008), http://websie.eclac.cl/sisgen/ConsultaIntegrada.asp; Bernardi *et al.* (2008).

implementing tax reforms and experiments, in search of an 'optimal' design. Many issues remain open in the debate and in the current design, such as fiscal federalism (see Afonso, 2001). These continuous changes make difficult a comparison between two years, as we have in Tables 5.1a and 5.1b. However, with the obvious *caveats*, the tables suggest interesting insights for the evolution of the tax structure in Latin American countries.

First of all, the tables make clear that the total level of tax revenue in Latin America has increased considerably, especially in Argentina, Bolivia, Brazil, Colombia, Nicaragua and Peru. These tax increases are the outcomes of economic growth, tax reforms, the improvement in tax administration and, in more recent years, for some countries (Venezuela, Bolivia, Chile and Mexico, for instance), an increase in revenue from government-owned natural resources, reflecting the boom in commodity prices.

Second, the tables show that the tax mix reveals a general preference for indirect taxes over direct taxes and social security contributions. In the last few decades the role of social security contributions has generally decreased, while direct taxes have increased and indirect taxes have decreased, mainly owing to the reduction of import and export duties.

Looking at the tax structure in more detail, Tables 5.1a and 5.1b show that personal income taxes are the most unexploited in Latin America, both in 1990 and in 2004. Their underutilization may depend on several factors (see Goode, 1972), among which are the large extension of the informal sector and a weak tax administration, which both have an impact on tax evasion. Tanzi (2008) argues that the low level of personal taxes mainly depends on the low or nil taxation of non-wage incomes (rents, interest, dividends, capital gains, profits), which often account for at least 70 per cent of the total personal income and are typically absorbed by the top 10–20 per cent of the population. According to the dominant view in Latin American governments, income from capital sources should not be taxed because of the fear of emigration of capital to other countries, the United States *in primis*. The effectiveness of these tax incentives has however been challenged by several experts (see Tanzi, 1966). In section 5.5 we propose additional explanations for this evidence.

Taxes on enterprise income have fallen over the period, mainly following a general trend of reduction and unification of the statutory corporate tax rates, although problems related to inflation and tax administration pose serious measurement difficulties. Extensive exemptions and tax incentives (see IBFD, 2006) still account for a considerable degree of tax erosion, though this has been decreasing in recent years (see in particular the experience of Argentina, which in the 1990s started to remove many tax incentive schemes). There is also a general trend towards simplification of corporate taxes, especially for small enterprises, the dominant ones in Latin America.

Property taxes are limited. This is quite surprising: since Latin American economies have a heavy agricultural sector and land ownership is still highly concentrated in most countries, we would expect strong pressures to redistribute land through land reforms or through high property taxes. However, on one hand high rates of inflation make it difficult to establish cadastral values for the land in order to facilitate the imposition of property taxes, while on the other hand political opposition from the landowners has played a major role.

On the contrary, value added taxes are now very important in the tax system of Latin American countries (see Ebrill *et al.*, 2001). In some of them they raise more than 10 per cent of GDP in revenue (see Table 5.1b). According to the so-called 'theory of tax structure change', domestic indirect taxes replace foreign trade taxes, especially taxes on imports, which were applied and important for countries with well-developed trade in the decades immediately after the Second World War. In the view of policy makers of that time, their main advantage was that these taxes could be exported, in the sense that they would be borne by the citizens of the countries that imported the commodities from Latin American countries. These export taxes almost disappeared at the end of the last century (see Tables 5.1a and 5.1b), with a few exceptions (see for instance Argentina), and they were replaced by VAT taxes. VAT started to be introduced in the late 1960s (in Brazil in 1967, Uruguay in 1968) and rapidly spread in the region. All Latin American countries now have a value added tax, and its level is often comparable to that of advanced industrial countries. VAT with a broad base and a single rate can be a very effective instrument of economic policy and a useful tool for stabilization because it is easy to estimate the impact of a rate change and to administer it. However, the application of VAT in Latin American countries has not always been highly productive (see Tanzi, 2008).

Finally, social security contributions have remained stable on average, and they account for quite low levels of GDP compared to advanced economies.

Having described the evolution of political regimes, the level of tax revenue and the tax structure of these countries, in the remainder of this chapter we will analyse the different relationships among them.

Summary statistics of all variables are in Table 5.2.

Table 5.2   Summary statistics of all variables

Variable	Observa-tions	Mean	Standard deviation	Minimum	Maximum
POLITY2	302	7.14	2.75	−7	10
DEMOC	304	6.14	11.07	−88	10
AUTOC	304	−0.93	10.11	−88	7
DURABLE	304	15.45	17.95	0	86
FREEDOM1	304	3.12	1.06	1	7
FREEDOM2	304	2.69	1.26	1	7
TAX_REV	304	13.72	4.15	1.40	26.20
DIRECT	304	3.58	2.12	0.50	15.70
PIT	199	0.62	0.58	0.00	2.40
CIT	231	1.70	1.76	0.00	14.30
PROP	304	0.40	0.49	0.00	2.20
TRADE	304	1.67	0.95	0.20	5.20
GS	304	7.71	2.82	0.90	14.80
SS	283	2.60	2.67	0.00	12.60
GDPVAR	272	1.15	3.88	−14.83	13.02
OPE	272	57.43	30.66	13.80	178.70
DEBT	280	53.62	45.74	8.17	304.50
AGR	281	10.82	5.95	3.40	34.10
OLD	304	5.35	2.21	3.18	13.52
FEMALE	304	48.71	9.56	30.20	68.20
URBAN	304	64.93	16.26	28.50	92.30
DENSITY	304	69.52	85.47	6.15	337.31
SCHOOLING	147	70.22	19.05	20.84	109.41
SHADOW	127	41.48	13.31	13.60	68.30
GINI	91	52.32	5.19	39.70	60.70
CREDIT1	37	0.21	0.14	0.01	0.69
CREDIT2	37	0.24	0.15	0.02	0.69

5.3 POLITICAL REGIMES AND TAX REVENUE

Tables 5.3a to 5.3g show the results of the regressions of our measures of the political regimes and economic variables on tax revenue.

As usual, in Table 5.3a to explain tax revenue we consider a set of fundamental economic variables (the growth rate of real GDP per capita, the share of the agricultural sector, the openness of the economy and the level of debt on GDP) and alternative measures of the political regime: the POLITY2 indicator (columns 1) and the two indicators of Freedom House, civil liberties (column 2) and political rights (column 3).[4] Column *a* reports the results without introducing time fixed effects and column *b* reports the result with them.[5] The political variables are significant in the expected way: more democracy, measured by a higher score of the POLITY2 indicator or by a lower score of the Freedom House indicators of civil liberties and political rights, is associated with higher tax revenue. As for the economic fundamentals, the openness of the economy is significant in the specification with a negative sign; the growth rate of real GDP per capita is positive and generally significant; the central government debt/GDP ratio is positive and significant, and the share of agriculture on GDP appears significant and shows a negative sign. The positive sign of the growth rate of income reflects the relation between growth and taxation (see also Figure 3.1); the negative sign of openness is mainly due to the reduction of tariffs and export duties, as we have already explained; the positive sign of debt is instead in line with the idea that a high debt will require high tax revenue; and finally the negative sign of agriculture follows the fact that the more agricultural a country is, the less it will have to spend for governmental activities and services (see Chapter 3). The same happens when time fixed effects are included.

Political variables remain significant with the expected sign[6] when we introduce the usual additional control variables: the share of elderly in the total population (Table 5.3b), female labour force participation (Table 5.3c), the share of urban population (Table 5.3d), the density of population (Table 5.3e), the level of education attainments[7] (Table 5.3f) and the shadow economy (Table 5.3g).[8] These variables have the expected impact: an older population, more female labour participation, urbanization, more education and a larger amount of the shadow economy are associated with higher tax revenue, while a higher density of the population is associated

Table 5.3a Tax revenue and political regimes: fundamental economic and political variables

	(1a) TAX_REV	(1b) TAX_REV	(2a) TAX_REV	(2b) TAX_REV	(3a) TAX_REV	(3b) TAX_REV
CONS	13.868	13.896	22.524	21.796	18.764	18.686
	(19.44)***	(9.18)***	(19.32)***	(13.13)***	(21.28)***	(11.85)***
GDPVAR	0.128	0.146	0.1	0.121	0.114	0.135
	(1.73)*	(1.97)*	(1.63)	(1.91)*	(1.52)	(1.81)*
AGR	−0.329	−0.313	−0.301	−0.289	−0.312	−0.289
	(−8.22)***	(−7.73)***	(−8.55)***	(−8.37)***	(−7.97)***	(−7.39)***
OPE	−0.013	−0.014	−0.022	−0.023	−0.01	−0.011
	(−2.78)***	(−2.80)***	(−3.57)***	(−3.68)***	(−2.19)**	(−2.23)**
DEBT	0.022	0.022	0.025	0.026	0.022	0.022
	(4.84)***	(5.24)***	(5.97)***	(7.28)***	(4.89)***	(5.54)***
POLITY2	0.452	0.431				
	(4.85)***	(4.30)***				

Table 5.3a (continued)

	(1a) TAX_REV	(1b) TAX_REV	(2a) TAX_REV	(2b) TAX_REV	(3a) TAX_REV	(3b) TAX_REV
FREEDOM1			−1.744 (−6.33)***	−1.866 (−6.67)***		
FREEDOM2					−0.756 (−3.83)***	−0.791 (−3.80)***
TIME FIXED EFFECTS		Yes (not signif.)		Yes (not signif.)		Yes (not signif.)
No. of observations	237	237	237	237	237	237
R^2	0.31	0.33	0.38	0.42	0.28	0.31

Notes:
All variables are explained in Chapter 7. Robust t-statistics in parentheses.
* Significant at 10%; ** significant at 5%; *** significant at 1%.
Regressions b include time fixed effects.

Table 5.3b   *Tax revenue and political regimes: the impact of the percentage of people over 65 years old (OLD)*

	(1a) TAX_REV	(1b) TAX_REV	(2a) TAX_REV	(2b) TAX_REV	(3a) TAX_REV	(3b) TAX_REV
CONS	9.723	9.1	14.035	13.723	10.76	10.265
	(11.21)***	(6.14)***	(9.07)***	(7.06)***	(9.09)***	(6.09)***
GDPVAR	0.095	0.114	0.088	0.108	0.092	0.112
	(1.66)*	(1.89)*	(1.58)	(1.86)*	(1.57)	(1.83)*
AGR	−0.222	−0.212	−0.225	−0.219	−0.217	−0.205
	(−5.59)***	(−5.17)***	(−5.88)***	(−5.67)***	(−5.48)***	(−5.07)***
OPE	0	−0.001	−0.005	−0.007	0.002	0.001
	(−0.1)	(−0.14)	(−1.2)	(−1.64)	(0.52)	(0.35)
DEBT	0.023	0.024	0.024	0.025	0.024	0.024
	(5.26)***	(5.65)***	(5.61)***	(6.44)***	(5.20)***	(5.64)***
OLD	0.768	0.766	0.669	0.631	0.82	0.802
	(6.69)***	(6.27)***	(5.10)***	(4.57)***	(6.98)***	(6.37)***
POLITY2	0.177	0.163				
	(2.47)**	(2.15)**				

Table 5.3b (continued)

	(1a) TAX_REV	(1b) TAX_REV	(2a) TAX_REV	(2b) TAX_REV	(3a) TAX_REV	(3b) TAX_REV
FREEDOM1			-0.729 (-3.05)***	-0.88 (-3.73)***		
FREEDOM2					-0.092 (-0.57)	-0.139 (-0.83)
TIME FIXED EFFECTS		Yes (not signif.)		Yes (not signif.)		Yes (not signif.)
No. of observations	237	237	237	237	237	237
R^2	0.46	0.48	0.47	0.5	0.46	0.47

Notes:
All variables are explained in Chapter 7. Robust t-statistics in parentheses.
* Significant at 10%; ** significant at 5%; *** significant at 1%.
Regressions b include time fixed effects.

Table 5.3c   Tax revenue and political regimes: the impact of female labour force participation (FEMALE)

	(1a) TAX_REV	(1b) TAX_REV	(2a) TAX_REV	(2b) TAX_REV	(3a) TAX_REV	(3b) TAX_REV
CONS	8.435	7.89	15.289	12.854	11.928	11.226
	(5.83)***	(3.27)***	(12.39)***	(5.99)***	(9.53)***	(5.11)***
GDPVAR	0.165	0.172	0.147	0.157	0.158	0.166
	(2.32)**	(2.40)**	(2.50)**	(2.67)***	(2.25)**	(2.35)**
AGR	−0.35	−0.351	−0.322	−0.342	−0.332	−0.332
	(−8.52)***	(−8.03)***	(−9.24)***	(−9.26)***	(−8.43)***	(−8.05)***
OPE	−0.004	−0.004	−0.012	−0.012	−0.001	−0.001
	(−1.05)	(−1.13)	(−2.47)**	(−2.67)***	(−0.2)	(−0.23)
DEBT	0.028	0.029	0.033	0.038	0.03	0.031
	(5.69)***	(5.78)***	(6.77)***	(7.70)***	(5.96)***	(6.21)***
FEMALE	0.104	0.103	0.137	0.158	0.125	0.125
	(4.26)***	(3.36)***	(5.87)***	(5.38)***	(4.89)***	(3.82)***
POLITY2	0.4	0.399				
	(4.75)***	(4.46)***				

Table 5.3c (continued)

	(1a) TAX_REV	(1b) TAX_REV	(2a) TAX_REV	(2b) TAX_REV	(3a) TAX_REV	(3b) TAX_REV
FREEDOM1			−1.866 (−8.21)***	−2.121 (−8.87)***		
FREEDOM2					−0.803 (−4.53)***	−0.857 (−4.44)***
TIME FIXED EFFECTS		Yes (not signif.)		Yes (not signif.)		Yes (not signif.)
No. of observations	237	237	237	237	237	237
R^2	0.35	0.36	0.47	0.5	0.35	0.37

Notes:
All variables are explained in Chapter 7. Robust t-statistics in parentheses.
* Significant at 10%; ** significant at 5%; *** significant at 1%.
Regressions b include time fixed effects.

Table 5.3d Tax revenue and political regimes: the impact of urbanization (URBAN)

	(1a) TAX_REV	(1b) TAX_REV	(2a) TAX_REV	(2b) TAX_REV	(3a) TAX_REV	(3b) TAX_REV
CONS	-1.31	-2.088	6.652	5.935	0.405	-0.197
	(-0.48)	(-0.67)	(2.40)**	(1.94)*	(0.15)	(-0.07)
GDPVAR	0.096	0.124	0.082	0.11	0.087	0.117
	(1.44)	(1.82)*	(1.38)	(1.82)*	(1.3)	(1.72)*
AGR	0.047	0.081	0.01	0.026	0.078	0.107
	(0.67)	(1.14)	(0.15)	(0.39)	(1.12)	(1.55)
OPE	0.015	0.016	0.004	0.003	0.018	0.017
	(2.80)***	(2.87)***	(0.78)	(0.53)	(3.67)***	(3.41)***
DEBT	0.015	0.015	0.018	0.019	0.015	0.015
	(3.78)***	(4.22)***	(4.60)***	(5.84)***	(3.76)***	(4.36)***
URBAN	0.17	0.176	0.144	0.144	0.179	0.181
	(5.78)***	(5.77)***	(5.31)***	(5.21)***	(6.33)***	(6.19)***
POLITY2	0.241	0.213				
	(3.39)***	(2.71)***				

Table 5.3d (continued)

	(1a) TAX_REV	(1b) TAX_REV	(2a) TAX_REV	(2b) TAX_REV	(3a) TAX_REV	(3b) TAX_REV
FREEDOM1			−1.183 (−5.52)***	−1.273 (−5.77)***		
FREEDOM2					−0.41 (−2.89)***	−0.436 (−2.81)***
TIME FIXED EFFECTS		Yes (not signif.)		Yes (not signif.)		Yes (not signif.)
No. of observations	237	237	237	237	237	237
R^2	0.42	0.45	0.46	0.49	0.41	0.45

Notes:
All variables are explained in Chapter 7. Robust t-statistics in parentheses.
* Significant at 10%; ** significant at 5%; *** significant at 1%.
Regressions b include time fixed effects.

Table 5.3e Tax revenue and political regimes: the impact of population density (DENSITY)

	(1a) TAX_REV	(1b) TAX_REV	(2a) TAX_REV	(2b) TAX_REV	(3a) TAX_REV	(3b) TAX_REV
CONS	14.449 (21.84)***	14.513 (10.04)***	22.189 (19.28)***	21.402 (13.35)***	18.822 (22.03)***	18.658 (12.46)***
GDPVAR	0.135 (1.86)*	0.165 (2.27)**	0.109 (1.76)*	0.139 (2.21)**	0.124 (1.68)*	0.157 (2.15)**
AGR	−0.277 (−7.52)***	−0.248 (−6.99)***	−0.26 (−7.48)***	−0.238 (−7.27)***	−0.257 (−6.86)***	−0.223 (−6.28)***
OPE	−0.012 (−2.56)**	−0.012 (−2.58)**	−0.02 (−3.39)***	−0.021 (−3.44)***	−0.009 (−2.04)**	−0.01 (−2.12)**
DEBT	0.018 (4.18)***	0.017 (4.72)***	0.021 (5.17)***	0.022 (6.74)***	0.018 (4.16)***	0.017 (5.00)***
DENSITY	−0.012 (−6.26)***	−0.013 (−7.23)***	−0.01 (−6.79)***	−0.011 (−8.67)***	−0.013 (−7.24)***	−0.014 (−8.58)***
POLITY2	0.399 (4.63)***	0.367 (3.98)***				

Table 5.3e (continued)

	(1a) TAX_REV	(1b) TAX_REV	(2a) TAX_REV	(2b) TAX_REV	(3a) TAX_REV	(3b) TAX_REV
FREEDOM1			−1.58 (−5.80)***	−1.663 (−6.05)***		
FREEDOM2					−0.68 (−3.68)***	−0.703 (−3.65)***
TIME FIXED EFFECTS		Yes (not signif.)		Yes (not signif.)		Yes (not signif.)
No. of observations	237	237	237	237	237	237
R^2	0.35	0.38	0.41	0.45	0.33	0.37

Notes:
All variables are explained in Chapter 7. Robust t-statistics in parentheses.
* Significant at 10%; ** significant at 5%; *** significant at 1%.
Regressions b include time fixed effects.

Table 5.3f Tax revenue and political regimes: the impact of schooling enrolment (SCHOOLING)

	(1a) TAX_REV	(1b) TAX_REV	(2a) TAX_REV	(2b) TAX_REV	(3a) TAX_REV	(3b) TAX_REV
CONS	4.055	1.737	10.858	8.369	6.242	3.657
	(1.95)*	(0.75)	(3.36)***	(2.71)***	(2.38)**	(1.43)
GDPVAR	0.121	0.113	0.126	0.14	0.118	0.116
	(1.45)	(1.22)	(1.56)	(1.52)	(1.39)	(1.23)
AGR	-0.014	-0.021	-0.031	-0.038	0.007	-0.002
	(-0.18)	(-0.28)	(-0.45)	(-0.54)	(0.1)	(-0.02)
OPE	-0.012	-0.007	-0.022	-0.018	-0.009	-0.004
	(-1.25)	(-0.75)	(-1.98)*	(-1.75)*	(-0.97)	(-0.46)
DEBT	0.02	0.022	0.023	0.025	0.02	0.023
	(2.87)***	(2.90)***	(3.05)***	(3.19)***	(2.85)***	(2.89)***
SCHOOLING	0.116	0.135	0.1	0.115	0.123	0.142
	(4.75)***	(5.43)***	(4.20)***	(4.56)***	(5.32)***	(5.83)***
POLITY2	0.287	0.274				
	(1.72)*	(1.83)*				

115

Table 5.3f (continued)

	(1a) TAX_REV	(1b) TAX_REV	(2a) TAX_REV	(2b) TAX_REV	(3a) TAX_REV	(3b) TAX_REV
FREEDOM1			−1.013 (−2.79)***	−1.03 (−2.78)***		
FREEDOM2					−0.371 (−1.35)	−0.309 (−1.18)
TIME FIXED EFFECTS		Yes (not signif.)		Yes (not signif.)		Yes (not signif.)
No. of observations	109	109	109	109	109	109
R^2	0.47	0.49	0.49	0.52	0.46	0.48

Notes:
All variables are explained in Chapter 7. Robust t-statistics in parentheses.
* Significant at 10%; ** significant at 5%; *** significant at 1%.
Regressions b include time fixed effects.

Table 5.3g   Tax revenue and political regimes: the impact of the shadow economy (SHADOW)

	(1a) TAX_REV	(1b) TAX_REV	(2a) TAX_REV	(2b) TAX_REV	(3a) TAX_REV	(3b) TAX_REV
CONS	10.096	10.885	20.794	20.957	17.131	18.018
	(6.16)***	(5.24)***	(14.02)***	(11.92)***	(12.82)***	(9.82)***
GDPVAR	0.102	0.094	0.064	0.07	0.074	0.066
	(1.03)	(0.88)	(0.91)	(0.88)	(0.72)	(0.61)
AGR	−0.284	−0.259	−0.273	−0.259	−0.264	−0.227
	(−3.51)***	(−3.22)***	(−3.63)***	(−3.47)***	(−3.11)***	(−2.70)***
OPE	−0.028	−0.028	−0.043	−0.043	−0.024	−0.025
	(−2.68)***	(−2.53)**	(−3.41)***	(−3.38)***	(−2.24)**	(−2.05)**
DEBT	0.019	0.019	0.022	0.024	0.02	0.02
	(2.14)**	(2.23)**	(2.77)***	(3.17)***	(2.17)**	(2.33)**
SHADOW	0.065	0.057	0.089	0.081	0.062	0.051
	(2.79)***	(2.10)**	(4.16)***	(3.31)***	(2.71)***	(1.94)*
POLITY2	0.687	0.672				
	(3.74)***	(3.22)***				

Table 5.3g (continued)

	(1a) TAX_REV	(1b) TAX_REV	(2a) TAX_REV	(2b) TAX_REV	(3a) TAX_REV	(3b) TAX_REV
FREEDOM1			-2.042 (-5.76)***	-2.152 (-5.83)***		
FREEDOM2					-0.858 (-2.61)**	-0.912 (-2.56)**
TIME FIXED EFFECTS		Yes (not signif.)		Yes (not signif.)		Yes (not signif.)
No. of observations	101	101	101	101	101	101
R^2	0.29	0.3	0.38	0.41	0.23	0.26

Notes:
All variables are explained in Chapter 7. Robust t-statistics in parentheses.
* Significant at 10%; ** significant at 5%; *** significant at 1%.
Regressions b include time fixed effects.

with lower taxes. All our control variables are significant and contribute to increase the explanatory power of our basic regression (R^2 increases from the range between 0.3 and 0.4 of the basic specification up to values larger than 0.5 in some specifications, and the F-test is in the standard range).

5.4 POLITICAL REGIMES AND THE STRUCTURE OF TAXATION

While the analysis of the determinants of tax revenue is in line with the general insights provided by the theory and by our overview of developing countries in Chapter 3, the analysis of the structure of taxation is far more interesting.

As we have already shown in Figures 5.3 and 5.4, Latin American countries are not characterized by the usual association between a democratic political regime and the level of direct taxes. The positive association between democracy and tax revenue is maintained but depends on the fact that indirect taxes increase more than direct ones. Thus there is no evidence of the effect of democracy on the mix between direct and indirect taxes.

Table 5.4 reports the regression results for the structure of taxation. We regress each source of the tax revenue (direct taxes, indirect taxes, trade taxes, social security contributions and property taxes[9]) on our fundamental economic variables, on the total amount of tax revenue and on our measures of democracy used (POLITY2, FREEDOM1 and FREEDOM2).

The regression analysis confirms that there is no evidence that more democracy is associated with more direct taxes. An opposite result emerges, that is more democracy is associated with less direct taxes and instead with more indirect taxes. This result on the mix between direct and indirect taxes is robust to all three measures of democracy.

Trade and social security contributions show insights quite difficult to interpret, since they are not robust to the three measures of democracy and they also show ambiguous signs: only POLITY2 is significant for trade taxes and with a negative sign, while less civil liberties seem to be associated with more social security. Property taxes are higher in more democratic contexts, where we could expect that the pressure toward taxation of landowners may be stronger.

Table 5.4   *Structure of taxation and political regimes*

	(1a) DIRECT	(1b) DIRECT	(1c) DIRECT	(2a) GS	(2b) GS	(2c) GS	(3a) TRADE
CONS	3.4	−0.23	2.142	−0.183	5.976	0.674	0.042
	(5.19)***	(−0.26)	(3.31)***	−0.26	(4.73)***	(0.76)	(0.16)
GDPVAR	−0.016	−0.013	−0.012	0.052	0.05	0.05	0.022
	(−0.44)	(−0.37)	(−0.33)	(1.37)	(1.33)	(1.33)	(1.84)*
AGR	−0.18	−0.174	−0.187	0.221	0.207	0.226	0.074
	(−8.03)***	(−7.99)***	(−8.61)***	(8.87)***	(8.27)***	(9.11)***	(7.90)***
OPE	0.006	0.011	0.006	−0.002	−0.014	−0.004	0.01
	(2.61)***	(4.08)***	(2.86)***	(−0.37)	(−3.59)***	(−0.72)	(10.52)***
DEBT	0	−0.002	0	0.003	0.008	0.004	0.005
	(0.17)	(−0.98)	(−0.01)	(1.41)	(3.19)***	(1.70)*	(4.01)***
TAX_REV	0.167	0.227	0.175	0.399	0.259	0.375	0.011
	(4.28)***	(5.43)***	(4.72)***	(7.23)***	(4.36)***	(6.81)***	(0.75)
POLITY2	−0.068			−0.019			−0.04
	(−1.66)*			(−0.31)			(−2.44)**
FREEDOM1		0.677			−1.242		
		(5.76)***			(−6.03)***		
FREEDOM2			0.281			−0.254	
			(2.73)***			(−1.75)*	
No. of observations	237	237	237	237	237	237	237
R^2	0.37	0.42	0.38	0.29	0.39	0.3	0.52

Notes:
All variables are explained in Chapter 7. Robust t-statistics in parentheses.
* Significant at 10%; ** significant at 5%; *** significant at 1%.

5.5   POSSIBLE EXPLANATIONS OF THE PUZZLE

Our result on the relationship between the political regime and the mix of direct *versus* indirect taxes is quite puzzling. According to the main political economy literature based on the median voter's theorem we would expect more direct taxes in more democratic contexts. Indirect taxes instead prevail in Latin America and thus inequality, which is *ex ante* very high, remains *ex post*. While these results may sound consistent with the non-democratic phases of the twentieth century, they are quite surprising after democratization.

In this section we explore possible political economy explanations

(3b) TRADE	(3c) TRADE	(4a) SS	(4b) SS	(4c) SS	(5a) PROP	(5b) PROP	(5c) PROP
0.133	−0.185	−3.531	−5.674	−2.874	−0.447	0.022	−0.184
(0.3)	(−0.58)	(−6.23)***	(−5.20)***	(−3.75)***	(−2.43)**	(0.09)	(−0.95)
0.023	0.023	−0.042	−0.039	−0.043	−0.018	−0.019	−0.019
(1.87)*	(1.93)*	(−1.28)	(−1.16)	(−1.35)	(−1.73)*	(−1.85)*	(−1.84)*
0.072	0.072	−0.056	−0.039	−0.05	−0.018	−0.018	−0.016
(7.63)***	(7.55)***	(−2.28)**	(−1.54)	(−2.05)**	(−2.79)***	(−2.80)***	(−2.54)**
0.009	0.01	−0.003	0.004	−0.001	−0.001	−0.002	−0.001
(8.12)***	(9.88)***	(−0.51)	(0.71)	(−0.26)	(−2.13)**	(−2.12)**	(−1.64)
0.006	0.005	−0.003	−0.006	−0.003	0	0	0
(4.30)***	(4.15)***	(−1.65)*	(−3.21)***	(−1.84)*	(−0.58)	(−0.37)	(−0.65)
−0.002	0.005	0.445	0.518	0.461	0.066	0.065	0.07
(−0.14)	(0.32)	(11.61)***	(11.78)***	(11.78)***	(7.08)***	(6.65)***	(7.48)***
		0.11			0.031		
		(3.02)***			(2.91)***		
−0.046			0.523			−0.072	
(−0.75)			(3.12)***			(−2.08)**	
	0.024			−0.074			−0.042
	(0.6)			(−0.71)			(−1.78)*
237	237	232	232	232	237	237	237
0.52	0.51	0.48	0.49	0.47	0.44	0.44	0.43

of this puzzling evidence.[10] These explanations can be grouped in two types: (i) the quality of the democracy suffers from low levels of representation, while vested interests or lobbying and interest groups play a crucial role, leading to economic outcomes rather different from the median voter's choices;[11] (ii) financial institutions, which are crucial for tax enforcement, have typically provided a low value added to Latin American firms which use them, and thus a high degree of 'disintermediation' characterizes these economies.

5.5.1 The Quality of the Democracy and the Role of Vested Interests

One of the main issues of democracy in Latin America concerns the quality of these political systems. The POLITY2 and Freedom House indicators capture some fundamental characteristics of a democracy. However, to what extent do these democracies have a substantial rather than a formal character? This would help explain why the economic outcomes are somehow different from the ones that would emerge in a true and well-consolidated democracy.

In a democracy, a small and homogeneous group of elected individuals are in charge to represent the large variety of public opinion and preferences. The quality of a democracy can thus be judged, at least in part, by the level of representation. In a democratic context, representation matters for the durability and stability of the democratic regime itself. However, the relation between representation and durability is not unambiguous. On one side, Diamond (1996) argues that under-representation may affect citizens' support for the system and thus increase the likelihood of a reversal to non-democratic forms of government. On the other side, as noted by Huber and Stephens (1999), in countries where poverty and inequality are prevalent, such as in Latin America, a lack of political representation may be associated with democracy consolidation, because, if subordinated classes are not represented, the elites can keep their interests more secure and reduce the possible threats of breakdown. However, once the economy develops, representation may increase without affecting the stability of the democracy.

The level of representation in a democracy may also play a crucial role in explaining economic policies. We expect that a democratic transition will not induce a significant increase in direct taxes, even in countries with the highest income inequality, when low-income groups are not enough represented, that is the representation level is low. Our countries lack in representation, a fact that may help to reconcile the evidence on taxation and formal democratic systems. Luna and Zechmeister (2005) build an index of 'mandate or issue representation'. Using data for 1997 and 1998 and considering the correspondence between party elites and party electorates on a variety of issues grouped in five areas (economic, foreign investment, religion, regime, law and order), they find the highest scores of this index in Chile and Uruguay, followed by Argentina. Colombia and Costa Rica stay in the intermediate range, and Mexico, Brazil, Bolivia and Ecuador are the less representative countries. The old democracies, Colombia and Costa Rica, seem to be characterized by only a shallow connection between elites and citizens (see in particular the experience of Colombia until 1974), but there is room for a significant improvement in the effectiveness of political representation in the young democracies too. In other words, there is room for these new democracies to acquire a more substantial character.

While in Latin American democracies political parties weakly represent voters' political preferences, they are largely influenced by the action of lobbies, elites and interest groups. In scarcely representative democracies, the government shapes policy more to the pressures of special interests than to the preferences of the general electorate.[12] The role of lobbies in the political process has been emphasized by Grossman and Helpman (1994). They argue that, once they have solved their internal free-rider problems, special interests groups can provide political contributions to influence the government's policy. The lobbying process can be seen as a two-stage non-cooperative game. Each interest group gives the government a contribution schedule that maximizes the aggregate utility of its members in which all possible policies are linked to specific contributions. Then the government chooses a policy and collects from each group the related contribution. The increasing ability to contribute and to deliver blocks of votes improves the position of special interests in the eyes of the government.

In general, one may underline that the threat of social unrest and revolution, as well as social pressure from the masses (Collier, 1999), was important to political elites introducing democratic institutions in Latin America (Argentina, Colombia and Venezuela). At the same time, social conflict has been responsible for democratic collapses and coups in this area of the world (O'Donnell, 1973; Stepan, 1985; Drake, 1996). In particular, political turmoil together with the alignment of interests between the elites and the military increased the opportunity to change political institutions from democracy to non-democracy. That's why democracy consolidation is so hard in Latin America (Argentina, Brazil, Chile, Guatemala, Peru, Uruguay and Venezuela). And that's also why actually, even in the presence of democratic political institutions, the power of the majority can be limited, for example, by the veto of the military over the decision-making process (e.g. Chile with Pinochet; Colombia is also one of the most consolidated democracies in the region but the system is often charged with a low representation of the interests of the majority).

Following this reasoning, taxation in Latin America may be seen as the result of the pressure of interest groups, which lobby to keep direct taxes low. In particular, the elites in power are generally the rich. They are interested in keeping down direct taxes not only for themselves, but also for the middle classes, in order to obtain their support in the political competition (see also Gómez Sabaini and Martner, 2008).

5.5.2 Financial Institutions

In a democratic system electoral terms and mandates impose a radical transformation of the temporal horizon. In this shorter time horizon, the appropriate time management becomes a top priority for the government. Financial institutions are developed in this direction, since they may allow governments to act as though they had infinite horizons at their disposal.

Once introduced and developed, financial institutions may also play a crucial role for tax enforcement. According to Gordon and Li (2005a), this role becomes very important in understanding why poor and rich countries have a different composition of the tax burden as a percentage of GDP. In poorer countries firms receive a lower added value (i.e. benefits) from using the financial sector than in richer ones. This affects the threat of 'disintermediation'. When firms depend on the financial sector, the government can obtain a lot of information about the scale of the firm's economic activity and use it to improve tax enforcement. Thus, the modest value added coming from the financial sector reduces the government's ability in a poor country to collect direct tax revenue.[13]

Following this reasoning, a possible explanation of the low tax burden in poor countries is that the underdevelopment of the financial sector, bringing about 'disintermediation', may be responsible for low tax enforcement and thus low revenue collection.

Moreover, if the benefits from using the financial sector are low, the design of the tax structure will be oriented towards a more intensive use of corporate income taxes, and tax collection will be focused on capital-intensive firms. This narrow tax base in fact depends more heavily on the financial sector and has a very low likelihood of 'disintermediation'. In this context, countries may also use an inflation tax as an instrument to raise the costs of cash transactions and create efficiency and revenue gains by improving the capital and labour allocation between taxed and untaxed sectors and shifting new firms to using banks as intermediaries. These results seem to be consistent with the Latin American context.

Gordon and Li (2005b) claim furthermore that this most intense use of taxes on corporate income in poor countries can also be justified using the lobby model of Grossman and Helpman (1994). Capital-intensive firms are interest groups actively lobbying to keep a low level of corporate taxation. When these firms are not numerous, such as in poor countries, they are not able to lobby effectively and, as a consequence, the level of CIT in the tax structure increases.

To conclude, a low level of representation, significant power of lobby and interest groups, and high 'disintermediation' from the financial sector which reduces tax enforcement are all important factors that explain why direct taxes remain low in the Latin American democratic context. Reducing the role of these factors seems to be essential to a democratic increase of redistribution which, lastly, would reduce inequality. This in turn may also have an important positive impact for growth and the overall development of Latin America (see Aghion *et al.*, 1999).

NOTES

1. These countries are a well representative sample of the Latin American region and they are all included in the CE PAL, OUS source of fiscal data for this region.
2. Notice that VAT in these countries may entail redistributive features. However, this is not likely to counterbalance the low level of direct taxes. Moreover, it is unclear why direct taxes remain low. We argue that this may be due to political reasons, as we will explain below.
3. Although we have mentioned that personal and corporate taxes have some specific features in the Latin American context, in the analysis, owing to lack of data, we have to refer to direct taxes, which include personal and corporate income tax, taxes on property and other direct taxes. We will mainly discuss the trend and determinants of direct taxes *versus* indirect ones. Indirect taxes include taxes on goods and services, taxes on international trade and transactions and other indirect taxes.
4. We do not consider the DEMOC or the AUTOC indicators from the Polity IV dataset because in Haiti and Peru the value of DEMOC is negative, owing to revolutions (see Polity IV dataset, 2007 for more details).
5. See Chapter 4 for our motivation about the introduction of time fixed effects.
6. The only exception is that democracy as measured by the Freedom House indicator of political rights is not significant when we control for the share of elderly and for educational attainment.
7. Notice that we here use an indicator of gross secondary school enrolment.
8. We have also controlled for the Gini coefficient and for the degree of development of the capital market. The results are qualitatively unchanged, although the number of observations is significantly reduced and thus we decided not to report the results.
9. Notice that direct taxes include personal and corporate income tax, taxes on property and other direct taxes. Indirect taxes include taxes on goods and services, taxes on international trade and transactions and other indirect taxes.

10. See also Tanzi (2008) on the role of the shadow economy and the decisive role of non-wage income.
11. Notice the opposite experience of the new EU members, in which the transition from an autocratic regime to a democracy is associated with an increase in taxes and public expenditures in line with the heritage of the former socialist regimes.
12. On the role of 'populist' policies see Acemoglu and Robinson (2006): populist policies are highly redistributive, but unsustainable. Thus, they are generally implemented by transitional (Peru, Argentina and Brazil) rather than established democracies (Venezuela, Colombia and Costa Rica), which are on the contrary associated with orthodox macro-policies (see Kaufman and Stallings, 1991).
13. Cash transactions are used here as a synonym of the informal economy, difficult to control and to tax. Firms that are not strongly dependent on the financial sector can rely on cash transactions, which do not leave a paper trail, in order to avoid (high) taxes (i.e. the cost of using the financial sector). This may increase the shadow economy.

APPENDIX TO CHAPTER 5: HISTORICAL NOTES

Argentina

In Argentina, serious economic problems, mounting charges of corruption, public denunciation of human rights abuses and, finally, the 1982 defeat by the UK in the Falklands War all contributed to discrediting the military regime that had been in power since the coup against Isabel Perón in 1976. In October 1983, Argentines went to the polls in elections found by international observers to be fair and honest, and the large turnouts for mid-term elections in 1985 and 1987 demonstrated continuous public support for the new strong and vigorous democratic system.

Bolivia

Bolivia returned to democracy in 1985 after 18 years of military dictatorship. In the 1990s, the politics of Bolivia referred to the presidents Sánchez de Lozada and Hugo Banzer. During his mandate from 1993 to 1997, Sánchez de Lozada and his coalition government implemented a series of social, economic and political reforms. The Banzer government continued the economic policies of its predecessor. However, after the third year of its term in office economic growth started to decline because of the financial crises in Argentina and Brazil and this contributed to increasing social protests against the government. In 2002, Sánchez de Lozada took office again, and in 2003 public tensions increased and culminated in the gas war that led the president to resign. He was replaced by vice-president Carlos Mesa, who was in turn replaced by chief justice of the Supreme Court Eduardo Rodríguez in June 2005. In December 2005, Evo Morales, the Socialist native leader, was elected president for a five-year term.

Brazil

The military maintained power in Brazil from 1964 to 1985 because of political struggles within the regime and local elite. In 1984 many public demonstrations held in the main cities made clear that military rule could not continue and that Brazilians were starting to require changes in the electoral system to directly elect their president. So, after the end of the military dictatorship, Brazil entered a troubled process of re-democratization, with the New Constitution in 1988 and the first direct presidential election won by Collor de Mello.

Chile

The Chilean military regime lasted until 1988, when in a plebiscite 55 per cent of the voters denied a second term to General Pinochet, the chief of a junta established by the army in power since 1973. The transition period started and President Aylwin, the candidate of the political coalition called the *Concertación*, received an absolute majority of votes in the 1989 elections, being in office from 1990 to 1994. After the two subsequent presidencies of the Christian Democrat Eduardo Frei Ruiz-Tagle and the Socialist Ricardo Lagos, in January 2006 Chileans elected their first woman president, Michelle Bachelet Jeria.

Colombia

In the mid-1960s, the Revolutionary Armed Forces of Colombia (FARC) and the smaller ELN (*Ejército de Liberación Nacional*) started their guerrilla insurgency campaigns against successive Colombian government administrations. In the mid-1970s, a new phase in the armed conflict against the state's authority and legitimacy came from the 19th of April Movement (M-19). From 1982 to 2002 there were four failed peace talks, the second of which incorporated into a peace process the M-19 and several smaller guerrilla groups and culminated in the elections of a Constituent Assembly that wrote a new constitution, which was promulgated in 1991. The current president, Uribe, during his first term in office (2002–06) implemented policies that reduced crime and guerrilla activity.

Costa Rica

The first truly free and honest elections in Costa Rica were held in 1889. Since then, only two brief periods of violence have interrupted the country's democratic development. The first was the Federico Tinoco Granados dictatorship from 1917 to 1919 and the second the Costa Rican civil war in 1948 which, once resolved, gave rise to the new constitution in 1949 and to the new democratic government. José Figueres Ferrer won the first democratic election in 1953. Since then, presidential elections in the country have been internationally considered peaceful, fair and transparent.

Dominican Republic

In the Dominican Republic, the election of the main candidate of the Social Christian Reformist Party (PRSC), President Balaguer, in 1994, was charged with fraud by the opposition Dominican Revolutionary Party (PRD). The subsequent Pact for Democracy signed by the competing political parties reduced President Balaguer's term of office from four to two years, set early elections and reformed the constitution. Leonel Fernández, the current president of the country, who belongs to the Dominican Liberation Party (PLD), won the 1996 elections and since then has run the government except for the period from 2000 to 2004 when Hipólito Mejía of the social democratic PRD was in power.

Ecuador

The election of Jaime Roldós Aguilera in 1979 represented a return to democracy after a decade of civilian and military dictatorships. Since then, in the country's administration, the centre-left parties alternate with those from the centre-right, both depending more on populist and charismatic leaders than on accurate and ideological programmes. Following the 1996 election, the indigenous population began to play an active and significant role in Ecuadorian politics, and in 1998 a specially elected National Constitutional Assembly established some constitutional changes.

El Salvador

Started in 1979, the Salvadoran civil war ended in 1991 under the Alfredo Cristiani administration. In 1992, the Farabundo Martí National Liberation Front (FMLN) became a political party in opposition to the Nationalist Republican Alliance party (ARENA), of which Cristiani was the leader. Since then, the last was the leading polity party of the country, for 18 years. However, in the 2009 elections, FMLN won with President Mauricio Funes.

Guatemala

The Guatemala civil war was the longest in the Latin American region, lasting from 1960 to 1996. At the end of 1996, thanks to Alvaro Arzú Irigoyen, the centre-right National Advancement Party (PAN) candidate, the peace process was concluded and peace accords between the government and the Guatemalan National Revolutionary Unity (URNG), the guerrilla umbrella organization whose general secretary was Comandante Rolando Morán, were signed. Since then, Guatemala has experienced democratic elections, the most recent in 2007 when Álvaro Colom, the candidate of El Partido Nacional de la Esperanza, won the presidency.

Haiti

After years of provisional governments and the ratification of the new constitution in 1987, Jean-Bertrand Aristide came to power in 1990 and started to implement radical populist policies. However, a year later, following a *coup d'état*, the military took the helm of the country. This regime, led by General Raoul Cédras, lasted till 1994, when Aristide was able to return. In 1996, René Préval succeeded Aristide in the first ever transition between two democratically elected presidents. They stopped being political allies later on, and a period of high political instability began till the intervention of an international peacekeeping force after Aristide's departure from Haiti. The interim government planned legislative and executive elections, which were held in 2006, and Préval took office for the second time.

Honduras

Following years of military rule, the country returned to civilian rule at the end of the 1970s. A new constitution was approved in 1982, and Roberto Suazo of the Liberal Party of Honduras (PLH) assumed power as the first constitutional president. He was succeeded by José Azcona in 1986 while, during the 1990s, Rafael Leonardo Callejas, the candidate of the rival National Party of Honduras (PNH), Carlos Roberto Reina and Carlos Roberto Flores were the subsequent presidents of the country. In 2005, after Maduro's government, the PLH came back to power. Its candidate Manuel Zelaya was inaugurated as the new president in 2006 and, after attempting to hold a non-binding national referendum, was arrested during the 2009 Honduras consti-tutional crisis. Since then, Roberto Micheletti, the former President of the Honduras Congress was appointed President by the National Congress for a term that will end at the beginning of 2010.

Mexico

The National Revolutionary Party (PRN), later renamed the Mexican Revolution Party and finally the Institutional Revolutionary Party, was in power from the end of the 1920s, determining what has been called an 'electoral authoritarianism' at both the state and the federal level. Minority parties began to be involved in the political system for the first time thanks to the 1970s reforms to the electoral system and the composition of the Congress of the Union. The first relatively free election was in 1994 when Ernesto Zedillo of the PRI won, even if with the lowest share of the vote ever for a PRI presi-dential candidate. The first opposition party president, Vicente Fox, was elected six years later in 2000.

Nicaragua

The longest military dictatorship in the country was that of the Somoza family, lasting for much of the twentieth century. During the 1970s, many Nicaraguans started to consider the Sandinista National Liberation Front (FSLN), founded by Carlos Fonseca and turning back to the historical figure of General Sandino, as the only hope for removing the brutal regime. The Sandinistas were in power from 1979 to 1990, when multi-party democratic elections led to their defeat and to the coming of Violeta Chamorro, the first woman president democratically elected in Nicaragua. In 1996 the Constitutional Liberal Party (PLC) won over Daniel Ortega and the Sandinistas, and the same happened in 2001, with President Enrique Bolaños succeeding Arnoldo Alemán. However, a change in the elec-toral law was decisive during the 2006 presidential election in allow-ing Ortega to return to power and start his second term in 2007.

Panama

In 1989 the US invaded Panama to remove Manuel Noriega, the leader of the country's military dictatorship from 1983. Guillermo

Endara thus came to power, but his government was unpopular and succeeded in 1994 by that of the party established by the military dictatorship. President Ernesto Perez-Balladares, a former official of the Noriega dictatorship, implemented many unpopular neo-liberal structural reforms, but failed to amend the constitution to permit him to run for a second term. The current president, Ricardo Martinelli, was elected in 2009, succeeding Martin Torrijos and Mireya Moscoso's government.

Paraguay

Paraguay was progressively isolated from the world community during Stroessner's 34-year reign, characterized by severe limitations of political freedoms and persecution of opponents. In 1989, Stroessner was overthrown in a military coup headed by General Rodríguez, who easily won the presidency in elections, instituted political, legal and economic reforms and initiated a rapprochement with the international community. A democratic system of government was then established by the 1992 Constitution. In 1996 the army chief, General Lino Oviedo, tried without success to oust the first civilian president, Juan Carlos Wasmosy. A period of political turmoil started with the next president, Raúl Cubas, who was elected in 1998 and resigned in 1999. Since then, the coalition government of President Luis González Macchi preceded those of Julio César Franco and Nicanor Duarte Frutos till that of the current president, Fernando Lugo.

Peru

Following the first Alan García government, in 1992, the elected president, Alberto Fujimori, gave life to an auto-golpe to exercise absolute authority in opposing the rural insurgent movement Shining Path, a fight that was characterized by atrocities committed both by the Peruvian security forces and by the insurgents and that became a symbol of human rights violations. Having revised the constitution and implemented substantial economic reforms, Fujimori resigned in 2000. In the new elections which were held in 2001, Alejandro Toledo, the leader of the opposition against Fujimori, came to power and started to restore some degree of democracy in the country after the authoritarianism and corruption of the previous governments.

Uruguay

In Uruguay, the unpopularity of the military government emerged in 1980 with the 'no' vote in the referendum proposing a change in the constitution. In 1984, after massive protests against the dictatorship, national elections were held and the new administration, led by Sanguinetti, started to implement economic reforms and to consolidate democracy. During his second term, following the government of Luis Alberto Lacalle, he continued Uruguay's economic reforms and integration into Mercosur, also trying to improve the electoral system and the welfare state. The current president, Tabaré Vázquez, came to power in 2005, following Jorge Battle, who defeated him in the election of 1999.

Venezuela

The beginning of the 1990s was characterized by political instability leading to two coup attempts in 1992 by Hugo Chávez against the Carlos Andrés Pérez government and his neo-liberal reforms. Following Octavio Lepage, Ramón José Velásquez and Rafael Caldera, Chávez was then elected president in 1998. He was the founder of the Fifth Republic Movement and the leader of the Bolivarian Revolution seeking to implement popular democracy, economic independence, and equitable distribution of revenues, and to reduce corruption in Venezuela. He was re-elected in 2000 and in 2006.

6. Asia, Latin America and new EU member countries

6.1 INTRODUCTION

This chapter reconsiders our two focus areas, Asia and Latin America, in a comparative perspective, having as a benchmark the new EU member countries that joined the European Union in 2004: Cyprus, the Czech Republic, Estonia, Hungary, Latvia, Lithuania, Poland, Slovakia and Slovenia.[1] Obviously, we are aware that each area presents its own history, background and institutional, economic and social characteristics which make comparisons very hard. However, we think that, with the necessary caution, some interesting insights may be drawn from jointly considering these transition areas. In particular, we consider this comparative perspective useful in shedding additional light on the relation between democracy and taxation in our two focus areas. In fact, the new EU member countries have all experienced a transition from a centrally planned to a market economy, they have become democratic and they have successfully implemented tax reforms during the transition period. According to the EBRD *Transition Report* (1999), central and eastern European countries, such as Hungary, Poland, the Czech Republic and Slovenia, have been the most successful in the transition, followed by Estonia and the Baltic states. Tax reforms are at the core of this good transition, although these countries are still experiencing some difficulties with the functioning of their new tax systems, mainly related to tax administration. What has determined this positive transition experience? And how can the governments address the remaining problems? We argue that political factors may play a crucial role.

In this world's area, the POLITY2 index ranges from a minimum of 6 in Estonia in the 1990s to a constant score of 10 for all of the considered period in Cyprus, Hungary, Lithuania and Slovenia, with small changes in the other countries, mainly on ascendant paths, in particular for Poland and Slovakia, which show the most pronounced increasing trends. These data suggest that these countries have more mature and stable democracies than those we considered in the other two areas of the world, Asia and Latin America. However, the political system even in the new EU member countries shows some element of political instability, as we will discuss further in the next section. Lobby and interest groups, for instance, play a relevant role in policy outcomes, and their action may contribute to determining the low efficacy of tax administration. These political economy issues make interesting a comparison across these areas of developing and emerging countries. However, the little variation in the democratic indicators that we observe for the considered period explains why we include this area only in a comparison with Asia and Latin America, while we do not develop a detailed analysis of this area of the world similar to that of the previous chapters.

The new EU member countries aimed at creating a tax system and tax administration not too different from those of the EU countries. Many studies have noticed that this objective was pursued without a clear road map, and in a context where the economic *status quo* was very different from that of the rest of the EU (Tanzi, 2005). However, many countries managed to successfully implement tax reforms: through early transition they have been able to avoid the fiscal crisis encountered by other transition economies, they have registered smaller increases in income inequality than other transition countries and they have shown a capacity in collecting tax revenue close to the EU levels. Still, their histories matter in the design of tax system and tax structure.

Fiscal data for new EU member countries are provided by Eurostat (2007, see Data Appendix in Chapter 7), a homogeneous source from 1995,[2] while data for earlier years are difficult to find and compare across countries. As a consequence, our analysis is restricted to the period 1995–2004.

Since new EU member countries represent a successful example of economic and political transitions and, in particular, of the implementation of relevant tax reforms, a comparison of the fiscal indicators of Asian and Latin American countries with those of the new EU member countries may thus be useful. We especially aim to understand whether transition countries are typically associated with larger tax revenue when their democracies are more mature and/or

what are the features of the structure of taxation, if any, which typically characterize democracies well after the transition period.

The chapter is organized as follows: in the next section we provide an overview of fiscal data of the new EU member countries, as well as a brief overview of some relevant political features. In the third and fourth sections we perform a comparative analysis based on the relation between our political indicators and the level of tax revenue and tax structure respectively, and we interpret our results as to how distant the outcomes of the Latin American and Asian countries are from the fiscal outcomes of the new EU member countries.

6.2   OVERVIEW OF TAX SYSTEMS AND POLITICAL FEATURES IN NEW EU MEMBER COUNTRIES

In this section we provide a brief, essential, though not exhaustive, overview of tax systems and political features in the new EU member countries, which will be used for the comparison with Asian and Latin American ones.

Before considering the fiscal data, we need to consider the main features of the tax systems in the new EU member countries and their development during the transition period. This brief overview will make clear that political issues have been important in the design of a new fiscal system during these years and that they still play a relevant role.

Before the transition, in this area of the world the role of taxes was not comparable to the EU one: most tax revenue was obtained from three major sources (corporation tax, in particular the tax on state-owned enterprises, turnover tax and payroll tax), while taxes on personal income were very limited. Tax rates were numerous, tax structure was complex and tax liabilities were discretionary and negotiable. Taxes were mainly collected on the basis of negotiations between the enterprises and the government. The presence of few taxpayers (mainly large enterprises) and the role of a mono-bank in processing payments did not require a well-functioning and efficient tax administration. There were no precise rules, codified tax law, well-defined tax bases and tax rates. As there were no explicit taxes, most individuals had no direct contacts with the tax authorities and they did not even know how much they were actually paying.

The transition made it necessary to radically change this tax system. The elimination of the planned economies implied that the government could not directly control quantities and prices to be taxed, and had to rely on tax declarations, which were not always correct owing to large-scale tax evasion. The main sources of revenues, such as tax on state enterprises, disappeared, while the number of new potential taxpayers largely increased owing to the birth of private sector activities. Also, corruption and bribes increased.

All these changes called for radical reforms (Tanzi and Tsibouris, 2000). A completely new tax system was needed, with a modern tax administration and taxes that could be enforced, with a stable revenue capacity. New fiscal institutions were essential to allow its correct functioning. Radical reform means not only that the new fiscal institutions have to introduce new instruments of taxation, a transparent, simple, efficient and fair fiscal system, and a well-working tax administration, but also that they have to correct attitudes, incentives and relations. In particular, the new fiscal institutions have to strengthen enforcement and at the same time develop the taxpayers' education and improve their compliance. This means that taxpayers have to be informed about the need to pay taxes and to be assisted in paying them, including through the simplification of procedures.

Tax reforms were implemented following an evolutionary country-specific approach, that is taking into account the economic and institutional constraints of each country rather than using a 'shock therapy' approach (OECD, 1991). Moreover, they were realized faster than in other transition countries, under the push of the accession to the EU. The Baltic countries in particular managed to adopt, in a relatively short period, new tax systems consistent with the best international standards and to reach considerable tax revenue levels. Obviously, the heritage of central planned past experiences still played a significant role, at least until the mid-1990s, in the design of these new tax systems, with provision of special treatments and incentives. However, as argued by Roland (2001), geopolitical factors helped in the process of overcoming these inheritances: transition represented an opportunity for these countries to shift from being satellite countries of the Soviet empire to being instead anchored to the European Union, adopting its political and economic system. People did not see this event as a traumatic experience, as for instance in Russia, but rather as a liberation. Governments such as the Czech, Hungarian and Polish ones entered a 'transition tournament', trying to show they were the most advanced transition countries in order to attract investments. This created favourable political support for reforms, especially in the field of taxation.

To raise revenues, that is to collect taxes, a political will is necessary, which is based on the support of citizens as voters (Burgess and Stern, 1993). However, to agree on policy decisions aimed at changing the composition of revenue, people need to believe and trust the efficacy and the fairness of the system. In the absence of this belief, people may choose not to support the policy, or not to pay. Thus, an adequate tax administration is necessary to guarantee an efficient extraction of resources. How the political system affects the ability to extract resources is a crucial issue. One of the main challenges for these countries is the risk of being stuck between the need to increase revenue, the weakness of the tax administration and the political difficulties of changing the status of tax policy in the absence of public positive belief in the system.

In fact, while tax policy improvements have been substantial, tax administration is still weak and fragmented. It was often created with a lack of financial resources, specialized skills and technical knowledge and a clear definition of strategies and objectives under a well-defined legal system. Political factors contributed to this low efficacy of the tax administration. On one side, political interference by powerful groups in politics and economics posed an additional constraint on the activities of the newborn fiscal institutions. On the other side, these institutions were created arbitrarily, rather than through a structured political process, and thus, owing to their lack of authority, they were even more exposed to these political interferences.

Moreover, widespread tax exemptions, deferrals and arrears indicate that the tax system is highly politicized, firms bargain with the state to obtain tax concessions and so on. In transition economies, it is not uncommon for firms to pay bribes to government officials in return for tax concessions and various favours. Obviously, the amount of these payments does not appear in government fiscal accounts. Interestingly, the EBRD (1999) and the World Bank construct a measure of the extent to which firms pay bribes to government officials: the average bribe tax in our transition countries ranges from 2.5 in Poland, to 2.8 in Estonia, 3.4 in Slovenia, 3.5 in Hungary and 4.5 in the Czech Republic. Again, the leading transition countries perform better than the others.

As a result, tax compliance is low and tax avoidance is high. An interesting study by Schaffer and Turley (2000) measures the effective tax administration in transition economies, by calculating the ratio between effective and statutory tax rates for 25 transition countries. This ratio is calculated for three taxes paid by firms: corporate income tax (CIT), value added tax (VAT) and social security tax (SST). Huge differences between effective and statutory tax rates indicate tax compliance and collection problems. The authors find that, owing to the greater politicization of the tax system, the shortfalls in effective tax yields in transition economies (calculated on 1997 data) are larger than a benchmark for mature economies (the 1996 average of the EU15 countries) where tax systems are well established, the administrative capacity is stronger and tax arrears are tolerated less frequently. However, the leading transition countries (Poland, Hungary, Slovenia, the Czech Republic and the Baltic states) have effective/statutory tax rate ratios similar to the EU average. Progress in transition, measured by an EBRD transition indicator, is positively correlated with effective tax administration, while countries with larger bribes have less effective tax administration, owing to a highly politicized tax administration. As stressed by Mitra and Stern (2003), this politicization of tax administration should be avoided. Political will plays an essential role in the administration of tax policy at two different levels: (i) to support the hardening budget constraints, and (ii) as a commitment to simplify procedures and tax regimes and to create an attractive investment climate. However, this does not imply that tax administration should be used for political ends, such as enforcing tax discipline on large taxpayers.

Additional political features are important for our analysis. All these countries have opted for a parliamentary regime, the main form of government in Western Europe, but they are still characterized by a certain political instability. Roland (2002) shows that Hungary and Slovenia have been very stable, with an average time between elections respectively of 48 and 47 months, while this time has been 32 months in the Czech Republic, 36 in Estonia and 36.5 in Poland. Average government duration has, however, been low (18.2 months in the Czech Republic, 12.9 in Estonia, 17.9 in Poland, 23.3 in Slovenia) with the exception of Hungary (48 months). Government duration between the two most recent elections has in general been longer (24 months in Poland and Slovenia, 48 in

Hungary) with the exception of the Czech Republic and Estonia (12 months), reflecting political tensions or instability. The average number of parties in government ranges from 2.2 in Estonia to 2.7 in Hungary, 3 in Slovenia, 3.2 in the Czech Republic and 3.4 in Poland, with a high percentage of right-wing parties in government. There is a huge variation in the re-election of incumbents: 50 and 100 per cent of re-elected governments respectively in the Czech Republic and Slovenia, with zero in the other countries considered by Roland.

Finally, we should notice that, as in other transition economies, in the new EU member countries interest groups and rent-seeking or economically and politically powerful groups still play a crucial role in determining policy outcomes, sometimes more than the political will of citizens as voters, including in tax reforms (Burgess and Stern, 1993; Roland, 2002). The support of powerful lobbies may be essential in implementing specific reforms which would never be approved by the majority of the people. In particular, owners of privatized enterprises, who represent a minority and are thus not likely to be pivotal in elections, may have incentives to organize as a lobby and exert their economic and political power to obtain tax advantages for their firms. Newly rich individuals benefit from many tax advantages and tax exemptions. Corruption is strictly related to the action of these groups. Finally, the action of powerful social networks, such as the Catholic Church and the Solidarity trade union in Poland, has been important in countering the Communist Party and in creating social support for the transition. In countries where these social networks did not exist, oligarchs and insiders emerged as a more powerful political and economic force.

The question of rent-seeking is also related to the distribution of wealth and power. The transition process increased inequality, with political and economic consequences. The increase in inequality affected the political decisions made through different political channels, which went beyond the median voter theory, including the relative role of electoral politics and special interest politics, and the policy and political coalition formation process. A vicious circle emerges when a few rich individuals are politically powerful: they can influence reforms in their favour, which in turn creates persistence for their economic and political power.

We are now ready to look in more detail at the fiscal data. Figures 6.1a and 6.1b show the evolution of tax revenue over the period 1995–2004 in the new EU member countries, and Tables 6.1a and

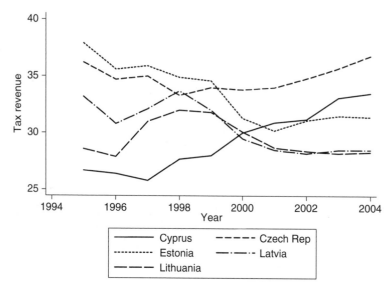

Source: Eurostat (2007), see Chapter 7.

*Figure 6.1a   The evolution of tax revenue (percentage of GDP) in
new EU member countries 1995–2004*

6.1b summarize the structure of tax revenue, comparing 1995 and
2004 data.

The incidence of tax revenue is now not much different from
the EU average, in many countries close to 40 per cent of GDP, in
some cases having come down from higher levels. As underlined by
Tanzi (2005), these levels are quite high with respect to the still low
per capita incomes, and it would be reasonable to speculate that
these burdens are likely to fall as the political and economic transformation of these economies goes on. As a consequence, public
spending is expected to be reduced. It should also be noticed that,
in spite of these high tax levels, all these countries, with the exception of Estonia, have developed high budgetary deficits, which have
been growing in recent years; that is, they have not yet succeeded in
reducing the role of the state to a level that can be financed through
ordinary tax revenue.

The mix between direct and indirect taxes is different from that of
the EU countries, with the new EU members still relying more than

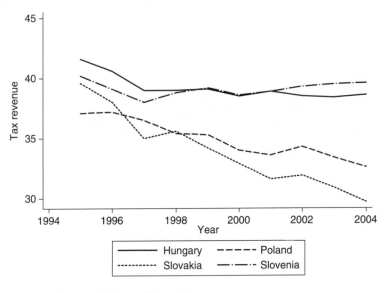

Source: Eurostat (2007), see Chapter 7.

Figure 6.1b   The evolution of tax revenue (percentage of GDP) in new EU member countries 1995–2004

EU countries on indirect taxes. Personal income taxes (PIT) are less progressive than in most EU countries, with flat-rate tax models often adopted (see the case of Estonia, in particular) and tax bases far from being comprehensive: capital incomes are typically taxed outside PIT under separate and preferential schedules, or are even tax exempt. This light capital taxation may contribute to the faster growth of the economies, but at the cost of low tax progressivity. On the contrary, in these countries the tax burden on labour is high, showing levels similar to those before the transition, with tax wedges close to the EU average for many new EU members. This is partly due to high levels of social security and welfare expenditures. Social security contributions are in some of these countries, such as the Czech Republic, among the highest in the world.

New EU members also apply very low corporate tax rates with narrow tax bases. This weak corporate taxation reflects the idea that enterprises, mainly small enterprises, are a key sector in promoting growth and employment. Mitra and Stern (2003) find a positive

Table 6.1a Structure of tax revenue (percentage of GDP) in new EU member countries in 1995

	Cyprus	Czech Rep.	Estonia	Hungary	Latvia	Lithuania	Poland	Slovakia	Slovenia
Direct taxes	8.8	9.6	10.9	8.9	7.1	8.7	11.7	11.5	7.1
Individual	3.9	4.8	8.3	6.7	5.3	6.5	8.4	3.7	6.0
Corporate	4.0	4.6	2.4	1.9	1.8	2.1	2.7	6.8	0.5
Social security contributions	6.5	14.3	13.1	14.9	12	7.4	11.3	14.1	17.3
Indirect taxes	11.4	12.3	13.9	17.8	14.1	12.4	14.2	15.1	15.9
Taxes on international trade and transactions	2.9	1.5	0.2	5.8	0.8	1.9	1.8	1.7	15.3
Tax revenue	26.7	36.2	37.9	41.6	33.2	28.6	37.1	39.6	40.2

Notes: Notice that taxes on property are not available. Direct taxes include personal and corporate taxes and other. Here taxes on international trade and transactions are other taxes on products (including import duties) in the indirect taxes category, which also includes VAT, excise duties and consumption taxes and other taxes on production.

Source: Eurostat (2007), see Chapter 7.

Table 6.1b Structure of tax revenue (percentage of GDP) in new EU member countries in 2004

	Cyprus	Czech Rep.	Estonia	Hungary	Latvia	Lithuania	Poland	Slovakia	Slovenia
Direct Taxes	8.7	9.8	8.2	9.1	7.9	8.7	6.4	6	8.5
Individual	3.5	4.9	6.5	6.6	6	6.8	3.7	2.8	5.9
Corporate	3.7	4.8	1.7	2.1	1.7	1.9	2.2	2.5	2.0
Social security contributions	7.7	15.0	10.7	13.3	8.7	8.4	13.5	11.9	14.7
Indirect taxes	17.1	12.0	12.5	16.3	11.9	11.3	13.1	12.5	16.4
Taxes on international trade and transactions	1.7	0.6	0.3	3.6	0.5	1.1	0.4	0.5	1.1
Tax revenue	33.5	36.8	31.4	38.6	28.5	28.3	32.6	29.7	39.6

Note: Notice that taxes on property are not available. Direct taxes include personal and corporate taxes and other. Here taxes on international trade and transactions are other taxes on products (including import duties) in the indirect taxes category, which also includes VAT, excise duties and consumption taxes and other taxes on production.

Source: Eurostat (2007), see Chapter 7.

correlation between the number of small firms and the level of development of the country. A major challenge for the governments of the new EU members is to create an attractive and competitive investment climate, which would give incentives to the activities of restructured and new enterprises. This challenge requires a clear political strategy, which includes reducing excessively high tax rates for small firms, simplifying regulatory procedures and tax administration for small firms and eliminating tax exemptions that benefit powerful special interests. All these measures would encourage compliance by small firms. A study by the EBRD (1999) finds that taxes and regulations are among the most important obstacles to the development of new enterprises in transition countries. Among the new EU members, Poland and Hungary have less complex systems of tax on business. However, tax incentives for new enterprises are currently almost zero in all countries, because of harmonization with the EU systems.

The share of indirect taxes is on the contrary quite high: all these countries have introduced value added taxes, which, with some adjustments, conform to the requirements of the European Union, and whose revenue covers the main share of indirect taxes. However, excise revenue and other similar taxes are still quite high, and many authors suggest that they will have to disappear in the future (Tanzi, 2005).

Finally, property taxes are still playing a marginal role, given that they were introduced a few years ago, with the diffusion of private property. They may however represent a crucial source of revenues in the future, especially to finance local governments.[3]

In general, while in the EU countries taxes on labour contribute more than half of total tax revenue, taxes on consumption less than 30 per cent and taxes on capital more than 20 per cent, in the new EU member countries the share of taxes on labour and of taxes on consumption is higher (2.2 and 6.3 percentage points respectively) and the share of taxes on capital is much lower (9.5 percentage points), as a result of the light taxation of capital income, but also of a large shadow economy and tax evasion. This last phenomenon in particular represents a serious problem for the fiscal development of these economies.

6.3   POLITICAL REGIMES AND TAX REVENUE

In this section we run a pooled OLS regression for tax revenue for a large sample of countries consisting of Asian (see Chapter 4),

The political economy of taxation

Table 6.2   Summary statistics of all variables

Variable	Observa-tions	Mean	Standard deviation	Minimum	Maximum
POLITY2	619	6.18	4.68	−7	10
FREEDOM1	613	3.22	1.40	1	7
FREEDOM2	614	2.81	1.71	1	7
TAX_REV	569	18.62	10.31	1.40	52.41
DIRECT	569	5.03	3.69	0.50	24.10
TRADE	556	2.07	2.12	0.01	15.30
INDIRECT	559	7.31	3.81	0.56	19.15
SS	445	4.67	5.03	0.00	18.60
LGDP	537	9.51	0.61	7.94	10.98
OPE	574	75.01	41.32	10.60	228.90
DEBT	551	50.05	39.00	2.49	304.50
OLD	624	7.08	3.75	3.18	16.59
FEMALE	624	53.41	12.25	28.80	79.50
DENSITY	624	251.60	872.03	6.15	6191.29
SHADOW	258	34.74	13.93	9.80	68.30

Latin American (see Chapter 5) and new EU member countries. We first include as fundamental economic variables the log of GDP per worker (LGDP),[4] the level of openness of the economy as a percentage of GDP (OPE) and the central government debt/GDP ratio (DEBT).[5] We also include our usual political indicators: the POLITY2 index, and the two indicators from Freedom House, civil liberties (FREEDOM1) and political rights (FREEDOM2). Two dummies capture whether a country belongs to the Asian or to the Latin American region. Table 6.2 contains summary statistics for all variables. The results are in Table 6.3a.

The standard association between democracy and tax revenue seems to be confirmed: more democracy, measured by any of our three indicators (i.e. a higher value of POLITY2 and a lower value of both Freedom House indicators), is positively and significantly related with more tax revenue as a percentage of GDP. Moreover, Asian and Latin American countries show significantly lower levels of tax revenue than new EU members.

Table 6.3a also provides evidence of the existence of an association between the level of income and tax revenue (see also Chapter 3), that is richer countries tend to have more tax revenue. Openness

Table 6.3a Tax revenue and political regimes: fundamental economic and political variables

	(1a) TAX_REV	(1b) TAX_REV	(2a) TAX_REV	(2b) TAX_REV	(3a) TAX_REV	(3b) TAX_REV
CONS	15.062	12.408	36.502	33.801	27.535	24.654
	(2.85)***	(2.37)**	(4.68)***	(4.48)***	(4.16)***	(3.84)***
LGDP	1.273	1.204	0.139	−0.024	0.798	0.664
	(2.06)**	(1.93)*	(0.18)	(−0.03)	(1.18)	(0.98)
OPE	0.011	0.01	0.01	0.009	0.009	0.008
	(2.27)**	(2.13)**	(1.89)*	(1.94)*	(1.78)*	(1.77)*
DEBT	0.006	0.006	0.008	0.009	0.01	0.01
	(1.33)	(1.49)	(1.90)*	(2.25)**	(2.31)**	(2.54)**
ASIA	−14.355	−13.895	−13.483	−12.82	−13.267	−12.658
	(−11.81)***	(−10.95)***	(−9.45)***	(−8.62)***	(−9.27)***	(−8.53)***
LATIN	−18.646	−18.165	−17.71	−17.133	−17.441	−16.874
AMERICA	(−29.90)***	(−26.73)***	(−23.62)***	(−21.84)***	(−23.14)***	(−20.82)***

Table 6.3a (continued)

	(1a) TAX_REV	(1b) TAX_REV	(2a) TAX_REV	(2b) TAX_REV	(3a) TAX_REV	(3b) TAX_REV
POLITY2	0.61 (5.98)***	0.588 (5.93)***				
FREEDOM1			−2.326 (−5.52)***	−2.385 (−5.67)***		
FREEDOM2					−1.848 (−5.62)***	−1.855 (−5.72)***
No. of observations	459	459	459	459	459	459
R^2	0.65	0.66	0.64	0.66	0.65	0.67

Notes:
All variables are explained in Chapter 7. Robust t-statistics in parentheses.
* Significant at 10%; ** significant at 5%; *** significant at 1%.
Regressions b include time fixed effects.

is also positively related with tax revenue (see again Chapter 3), while the level of debt shows no significant association with tax revenue. Finally, all these results are robust to the inclusion of time fixed effects.

We then enrich our basic specification by introducing the usual additional control variables in Tables 6.3b to 6.3f (see Chapter 3).[6]

In Table 6.3b we include the share of elderly in the population (OLD), which turns out to be significantly and positively related to the level of tax revenue. The political variables are still significant, as well as the dummy variables for Asian and Latin American countries. The same result is obtained in Table 6.3c, where we control for the female labour force participation rate (FEMALE), which significantly explains part of the tax revenue across countries, but does not alter the significance of the political variables, nor the difference between Asian (and Latin American) and new EU member countries. In Table 6.3d we control for the density of the population (DENSITY), which turns out to be negatively and significantly related to the level of tax revenue. The political variables are robust both to this inclusion and to that of the level of the shadow economy (SHADOW) in Table 6.3e, which is positively and significantly related to the level of tax revenue. Finally, in Table 6.3f we include all control variables together: being an Asian country or a Latin American one explains to some extent the lower tax revenue with respect to new EU member countries, but more democracy is still associated with more tax revenue, using any of the three political indicators. This result can be interpreted as a support for the hypothesis that transition countries, which are able to develop more mature and more stable democracies, tend to have a larger tax system, measured as tax revenue as a percentage of GDP.

6.4   POLITICAL REGIMES AND THE STRUCTURE OF TAXATION

In this section we turn to the analysis of the tax structure. While the association between the democratic indicators and the level of tax revenue is always robust, as confirmed by the previous section and the previous chapters, the results of the analysis of the tax structure have a more difficult interpretation. According to data availability,

Table 6.3b   Tax revenue and political regimes: the impact of the percentage of people over 65 years old (OLD)

	(1a) TAX_REV	(1b) TAX_REV	(2a) TAX_REV	(2b) TAX_REV	(3a) TAX_REV	(3b) TAX_REV
CONS	18.204	15.261	37.548	35.008	29.105	26.066
	(3.63)***	(3.07)***	(4.85)***	(4.73)***	(4.55)***	(4.24)***
LGDP	0.128	0.204	−0.58	−0.654	0.04	0.046
	(0.22)	(0.35)	(−0.83)	(−0.94)	(0.07)	(0.08)
OPE	0.015	0.014	0.012	0.012	0.012	0.011
	(3.24)***	(3.11)***	(2.43)**	(2.48)**	(2.39)**	(2.35)**
DEBT	0.009	0.009	0.011	0.011	0.012	0.012
	(2.08)**	(2.20)**	(2.46)**	(2.80)***	(2.87)***	(3.05)***
OLD	0.585	0.518	0.421	0.365	0.42	0.346
	(4.05)***	(3.21)***	(2.48)**	(1.99)**	(2.51)**	(1.88)*
ASIA	−10.441	−10.49	−10.853	−10.559	−10.631	−10.516
	(−8.82)***	(−8.56)***	(−8.57)***	(−8.11)***	(−8.53)***	(−8.23)***
LATIN AMERICA	−14.435	−14.502	−14.782	−14.626	−14.522	−14.502
	(−12.00)***	(−11.37)***	(−11.39)***	(−10.94)***	(−11.73)***	(−11.16)***

	(1)	(2)	(3)	(4)	(5)	(6)
POLITY2	0.611 (5.96)***	0.593 (5.95)***				
FREEDOM1			−2.216 (−4.93)***	−2.313 (−5.20)***		
FREEDOM2					−1.773 (−5.09)***	−1.802 (−5.25)***
No. of observations	459	459	459	459	459	459
R^2	0.66	0.67	0.65	0.66	0.66	0.67

Notes:
All variables are explained in Chapter 7. Robust t-statistics in parentheses.
* Significant at 10%; ** significant at 5%; *** significant at 1%.
Regressions b include time fixed effects.

151

Table 6.3c Tax revenue and political regimes: the impact of female labour force participation (FEMALE)

	(1a) TAX_REV	(1b) TAX_REV	(2a) TAX_REV	(2b) TAX_REV	(3a) TAX_REV	(3b) TAX_REV
CONS	−0.839	−2.434	24.383	22.846	13.718	11.8
	(−0.15)	(−0.43)	(3.18)***	(3.03)***	(2.07)**	(1.79)*
LGDP	1.603	1.551	0.344	0.148	1.068	0.946
	(2.56)**	(2.44)**	(0.46)	(0.2)	(1.57)	(1.37)
OPE	0.007	0.006	0.005	0.006	0.004	0.005
	(1.42)	(1.37)	(1.07)	(1.22)	(0.88)	(0.95)
DEBT	0.025	0.024	0.026	0.027	0.029	0.029
	(5.02)***	(5.19)***	(5.22)***	(5.77)***	(5.96)***	(6.34)***
FEMALE	0.188	0.179	0.171	0.168	0.184	0.176
	(8.43)***	(8.09)***	(8.38)***	(8.38)***	(8.49)***	(8.17)***
ASIA	−12.11	−11.907	−11.446	−10.859	−10.962	−10.566
	(−10.02)***	(−9.60)***	(−7.93)***	(−7.29)***	(−7.60)***	(−7.20)***
LATIN	−16.386	−16.179	−15.592	−15.141	−15.077	−14.738
AMERICA	(−22.59)***	(−21.94)***	(−18.89)***	(−18.22)***	(−17.89)***	(−17.21)***

POLITY2	0.71 (7.19)***	0.692 (7.17)***			
FREEDOM1			−2.593 (−6.34)***	−2.73 (−6.61)***	
FREEDOM2					−2.114 (−6.60)***	−2.14 (−6.79)***
No. of observations	459	459	459	459	459	459
R^2	0.68	0.69	0.67	0.68	0.68	0.69

Notes:
All variables are explained in Chapter 7. Robust t-statistics in parentheses.
* Significant at 10%; ** significant at 5%; *** significant at 1%.
Regressions b include time fixed effects.

Table 6.3d   Tax revenue and political regimes: the impact of population density (DENSITY)

	(1a) TAX_REV	(1b) TAX_REV	(2a) TAX_REV	(2b) TAX_REV	(3a) TAX_REV	(3b) TAX_REV
CONS	8.698	6.049	26.984	24.68	19.171	16.524
	(1.62)	(1.12)	(3.62)***	(3.39)***	(3.05)***	(2.67)***
LGDP	1.799	1.728	0.847	0.663	1.404	1.261
	(2.96)***	(2.80)***	(1.17)	(0.91)	(2.19)**	(1.95)*
OPE	0.028	0.027	0.027	0.026	0.029	0.028
	(3.59)***	(3.54)***	(3.68)***	(3.69)***	(3.83)***	(3.78)***
DEBT	0.01	0.01	0.012	0.013	0.014	0.014
	(2.28)**	(2.49)**	(2.83)***	(3.19)***	(3.29)***	(3.60)***
DENSITY	−0.002	−0.002	−0.002	−0.002	−0.002	−0.002
	(−3.92)***	(−3.89)***	(−4.59)***	(−4.51)***	(−5.10)***	(−4.96)***
ASIA	−13.234	−12.795	−12.471	−11.858	−11.953	−11.393
	(−10.24)***	(−9.51)***	(−8.55)***	(−7.84)***	(−7.97)***	(−7.35)***
LATIN AMERICA	−17.834	−17.376	−17.009	−16.472	−16.572	−16.047
	(−24.83)***	(−22.51)***	(−21.30)***	(−19.78)***	(−19.87)***	(−18.01)***

POLITY2	0.537 (5.41)***	0.517 (5.33)***			
FREEDOM1			−2.012 (−4.98)***	−2.085 (−5.13)***	
FREEDOM2				−1.668 (−5.32)***	−1.685 (−5.43)***
No. of observations	459	459	459	459	459
R^2	0.66	0.67	0.65	0.67	0.66

Notes:
All variables are explained in Chapter 7. Robust t-statistics in parentheses.
* Significant at 10%; ** significant at 5%; *** significant at 1%.
Regressions b include time fixed effects.

Table 6.3e   Tax revenue and political regimes: the impact of the shadow economy (SHADOW)

	(1a) TAX_REV	(1b) TAX_REV	(2a) TAX_REV	(2b) TAX_REV	(3a) TAX_REV	(3b) TAX_REV
CONS	−7.996	−6.694	3.395	7.27	−1.713	1.452
	(−0.81)	(−0.67)	(0.29)	(0.61)	(−0.15)	(0.13)
LGDP	3.438	3.038	2.991	2.351	3.342	2.743
	(3.15)***	(2.66)***	(2.61)***	(1.95)*	(3.00)***	(2.30)**
OPE	−0.005	−0.004	−0.007	−0.005	−0.007	−0.005
	(−0.69)	(−0.54)	(−0.92)	(−0.62)	(−0.94)	(−0.68)
DEBT	0.012	0.012	0.013	0.013	0.015	0.015
	(1.63)	(1.77)*	(1.92)*	(2.21)**	(2.07)**	(2.31)**
SHADOW	0.168	0.147	0.182	0.159	0.171	0.143
	(4.99)***	(4.37)***	(5.42)***	(4.88)***	(5.30)***	(4.33)***
ASIA	−13.81	−13.451	−13.436	−12.745	−13.316	−12.647
	(−7.16)***	(−6.77)***	(−6.46)***	(−5.87)***	(−6.11)***	(−5.55)***
LATIN	−21.048	−20.461	−20.674	−19.849	−20.327	−19.435
AMERICA	(−20.61)***	(−19.23)***	(−18.67)***	(−17.88)***	(−17.09)***	(−15.24)***

	(1)	(2)	(3)	(4)	(5)	(6)
POLITY2	0.437 (2.65)***	0.449 (2.70)***				
FREEDOM1			-1.593 (-2.79)***	-1.845 (-3.05)***		
FREEDOM2					-1.18 (-2.48)**	-1.333 (-2.68)***
No. of observations	191	191	191	191	191	191
R^2	0.65	0.66	0.65	0.66	0.65	0.66

Notes:
All variables are explained in Chapter 7. Robust t-statistics in parentheses.
* Significant at 10%; ** significant at 5%; *** significant at 1%.
Regressions b include time fixed effects.

Table 6.3f Tax revenue and political regimes: all control variables

	(1a) TAX_REV	(1b) TAX_REV	(2a) TAX_REV	(2b) TAX_REV	(3a) TAX_REV	(3b) TAX_REV
CONS	−21.697	−18.354	−11.782	−8.299	−16.709	−11.227
	(−2.06)**	(−1.70)*	(−1.11)	(−0.77)	(−1.59)	(−1.02)
LGDP	3.936	3.631	4.056	3.498	4.191	3.711
	(3.35)***	(3.07)***	(3.49)***	(3.00)***	(3.62)***	(3.24)***
OPE	0.008	0.01	0.003	0.006	0.007	0.01
	(0.7)	(0.92)	(0.24)	(0.51)	(0.61)	(0.88)
DEBT	0.029	0.028	0.031	0.032	0.033	0.033
	(3.35)***	(3.35)***	(4.15)***	(4.50)***	(3.85)***	(3.93)***
OLD	−0.145	−0.131	−0.434	−0.439	−0.305	−0.305
	(−0.48)	(−0.42)	(−1.16)	(−1.14)	(−0.89)	(−0.86)
FEMALE	0.157	0.149	0.175	0.174	0.167	0.16
	(4.22)***	(4.15)***	(4.17)***	(4.27)***	(4.13)***	(4.19)***
DENSITY	−0.001	−0.002	−0.001	−0.002	−0.002	−0.002
	(−2.59)**	(−2.73)***	(−2.83)***	(−2.99)***	(−3.35)***	(−3.46)***
SHADOW	0.127	0.114	0.144	0.126	0.126	0.105
	(3.90)***	(3.48)***	(4.33)***	(3.89)***	(4.06)***	(3.28)***

	(1)	(2)	(3)	(4)	(5)	(6)
ASIA	−12.184	−11.839	−13.279	−12.6	−12.243	−11.674
	(−6.38)***	(−6.08)***	(−7.33)***	(−6.99)***	(−6.31)***	(−5.90)***
LATIN AMERICA	−19.304	−18.804	−20.764	−20.046	−19.323	−18.61
	(−7.95)***	(−7.67)***	(−7.91)***	(−7.87)***	(−7.90)***	(−7.64)***
POLITY2	0.48	0.483				
	(3.21)***	(3.18)***				
FREEDOM1			−1.944	−2.23		
			(−2.97)***	(−3.22)***		
FREEDOM2					−1.393	−1.524
					(−2.86)***	(−3.02)***
No. of observations	191	191	191	191	191	191
R^2	0.68	0.69	0.68	0.69	0.68	0.69

Notes:
All variables are explained in Chapter 7. Robust t-statistics in parentheses.
* Significant at 10%; ** significant at 5%; *** significant at 1%.
Regressions b include time fixed effects.

Table 6.4a   Structure of taxation and political regimes: direct taxes

	(1) DIRECT	(2) DIRECT	(3) DIRECT
CONS	−3.339	−0.308	−0.643
	(−1.05)	(−0.08)	(−0.19)
LGDP	0.876	0.794	0.791
	(2.64)**	(2.16)*	(2.33)*
OPE	0.019	0.019	0.019
	(4.71)***	(4.71)***	(4.86)***
DEBT	−0.002	−0.001	−0.001
	(−0.61)	(−0.25)	(−0.26)
ASIA	−0.972	−0.982	−0.675
	(−1.94)*	(−1.84)*	(−1.27)
LATIN AMERICA	−3.942	−3.811	−3.594
	(−9.2)***	(−8.59)***	(−8.08)***
POLITY2	0.16		
	(4.07)***		
FREEDOM1		−0.421	
		(−2.6)*	
FREEDOM2			−0.453
			(−3.95)***
No. of observations	440	440	440
R^2	0.42	0.40	0.41

Notes:
All variables are explained in Chapter 7. Robust t-statistics in parentheses.
* Significant at 10%; ** significant at 5%; *** significant at 1%.

we perform the analysis separately for direct taxes (which include personal income taxes, corporate income and other direct taxes), indirect taxes, social security and trade taxes.[7] The results are in Tables 6.4a, 6.4b, 6.4c and 6.4d.

Table 6.4a shows the result of an OLS regression of the total amount of direct taxes[8] on the economic and political fundamentals, which include the log of GDP per worker, the openness of the economy, the level of debt as a percentage of GDP and an indicator of democracy (POLITY2 and the two indexes calculated by Freedom House respectively). More democracy (a higher score of POLITY2 or a lower score of FREEDOM1 and FREEDOM2) is associated with more direct taxes. Asian and Latin American coun-

Table 6.4b Structure of taxation and political regimes: indirect taxes

	(1) INDIRECT	(2) INDIRECT	(3) INDIRECT
CONS	10.670	23.668	15.472
	(2.98)**	(5.81)***	(4.13)***
LGDP	−0.142	−1.076	−0.437
	(−0.38)	(−2.73)**	(−1.16)
OPE	0.005	0.004	0.006
	(1.16)	(0.95)	(1.31)
DEBT	0.001	0	0.002
	(0.31)	(0.12)	(0.45)
ASIA	−3.55	−2.551	−2.86
	(−6.14)***	(−4.39)***	(−4.76)***
LATIN AMERICA	−4.613	−4.021	−4.052
	(−9.2)***	(−8.15)***	(−7.91)***
POLITY2	0.14		
	(3.19)**		
FREEDOM1		−1.153	
		(−6.66)***	
FREEDOM2			−0.611
			(−4.82)***
No. of observations	434	434	434
R^2	0.26	0.32	0.28

Notes:
All variables are explained in Chapter 7. Robust t-statistics in parentheses.
* Significant at 10%; ** significant at 5%; *** significant at 1%.

tries show a significantly lower level of direct taxes than new EU member countries.

Table 6.4b refers instead to indirect taxes: more democracy is also significantly associated with a higher level of indirect taxes. The results of Tables 6.4a and 6.4b together suggest that there is no evidence in our sample of transition countries of a trade-off between direct and indirect taxes. More democratic countries are indeed associated with higher tax revenue (see section 6.3) owing to a higher share of both direct and indirect taxes. In transition countries not only direct but also indirect taxes may in general entail some element of redistribution (for the specific case of Latin America, see Bernardi

Table 6.4c   *Structure of taxation and political regimes: social security contributions*

	(1) SS	(2) SS	(3) SS
CONS	1.697	−0.747	2.902
	(0.55)	(−0.27)	(0.96)
LGDP	1.017	1.333	1.031
	(3.24)***	(4.53)***	(3.24)***
OPE	−0.006	−0.005	−0.006
	(−1.45)	(−1.25)	(−1.35)
DEBT	0	0	0
	(−0.13)	(0.1)	(0.15)
ASIA	−11.108	−11.725	−11.081
	(−32.45)***	(−30.17)***	(−27.43)***
LATIN AMERICA	−9.229	−9.447	−9.083
	(−21.42)***	(−21.36)***	(−19.34)***
POLITY2	0.124		
	(3.81)***		
FREEDOM1		0.162	
		(1)	
FREEDOM2			−0.243
			(−2.55)**
No. of observations	362	362	362
R^2	0.76	0.75	0.76

Notes:
All variables are explained in Chapter 7. Robust t-statistics in parentheses.
* Significant at 10%; ** significant at 5%; *** significant at 1%.

et al., 2008) and, since indirect taxes are easier to manage, especially in non-mature democracies, it may be a good strategy to achieve redistribution through indirect taxation. Somewhat surprisingly, Asian and Latin American countries, less mature democracies, show a significantly lower level of indirect taxes than new EU member countries.

Table 6.4c shows that there is no clear result when we analyse the association between the level of social security contributions and the political regime. Asian and Latin American countries have certainly a smaller level of social security contributions than new EU member countries, but the role played by the democratic

Table 6.4d   Structure of taxation and political regimes: trade taxes

	(1) TRADE	(2) TRADE	(3) TRADE
CONS	7.747	12.671	10.509
	(5.42)***	(5.82)***	(5.75)***
LGDP	−0.771	−0.97	−0.813
	(−4.34)***	(−4.24)***	(−4.06)***
OPE	0.003	0.002	0.002
	(2.43)**	(1.35)	(1.3)
debt	0.006	0.007	0.008
	(4.67)***	(5.16)***	(5.49)***
ASIA	0.751	0.743	0.814
	(1.76)*	(1.47)	(1.68)*
LATIN AMERICA	−0.704	−0.578	−0.49
	(−1.91)*	(−1.39)	(−1.22)
POLITY 2	0.192		
	(7.94)***		
FREEDOM 1		−0.562	
		(−5.38)***	
FREEDOM 2			−0.452
			(−5.64)***
No. of observations	451	451	451
R^2	0.18	0.14	0.15

Notes:
All variables are explained in Chapter 7. Robust t-statistics in parentheses.
* Significant at 10%; ** significant at 5%; *** significant at 1%.

institutions is not unambiguous, since it depends on the indicator of democracy that we use. Following the predictions of the political economy standard models, we expect more democracies to be associated with more social security. While this result is confirmed using the POLITY2 indicator and the Freedom House index of political rights, it is not confirmed using the Freedom House indicator of civil liberties. We interpret this finding as evidence that the association between democracy and the level of social security is not robust.[9] Finally, Table 6.4d also shows that taxes on trade are larger in more democratic countries and that the specific area does not matter (or matters weakly in specific cases) in determining the level of these taxes.

6.5 CONCLUSIONS

This chapter has performed a comparative analysis of tax systems in Asian and Latin American countries with respect to new EU members. Though the new EU member countries show better indicators of democracy (POLITY2 in particular) than countries in the other two areas of the world, and more stable values, their recent transition shares with these countries some political difficulties. In particular, interest groups have often played against a correct functioning of tax administration, which is essential for the implementation of effective tax reforms.

Our comparative analysis has shown that the lower scores of democratization in Asia and Latin America are associated with lower tax revenue with respect to the values of the new EU members. This result is robust to the inclusion of several control variables. We have also found that more democracy is associated with more direct taxes and with more indirect taxes. Since in developing countries not only direct but also indirect taxes may induce redistribution, the standard association between democracy and redistribution predicted by political economy models (see Chapter 2) seems to be confirmed. The association between democracy and the level of social security contributions is however not significant.

NOTES

1. We do not consider Malta because the country is not in the Polity IV dataset.
2. From 1995, the ESA95 was adopted.
3. One of the main challenges for these countries, such as the Czech Republic and Hungary, is the definition of government responsibilities at the local level, including details of revenue and expenditure assignments. In these countries the role of intermediate levels of government is now relatively clear, but the role of the local governments is still problematic, with problems of fragmented or inefficient service delivery. Local governments need greater accountability, to collect their own sources of revenue and make decisions with greater autonomy over them. In this respect, local taxes could play a crucial role.
4. Since we here consider very different countries, we need to control for GDP.
5. We do not include the share of agriculture on GDP (AGR) owing to a lack of data from homogeneous sources.
6. We do not include the share of urban population (URBAN) owing to lack of data from homogeneous sources. Even in these cases, our results do not change if time fixed effects are included in the analysis.
7. Notice that the specific items that compose total direct and total indirect taxes have been classified using a homogeneous criterion for all countries so that we

have comparable categories. We do not consider property taxes owing to a lack of data for new EU members. Notice also that our results on the significant impact of political variables on direct and indirect taxes are not sensitive to the specific reclassification of items in the two categories of direct and indirect that we have used.

8. We decided not to show the results with PIT and CIT separately, since for Latin American countries the detailed data are not always available (see Chapter 5). Notice however that new EU members typically show a higher level of personal income taxes (in the new EU member countries the level is not far from the EU average and the average level of developed economies) than the other developing countries. This result is in line with the evidence that more mature democracies have high levels of redistribution and tend to tax more personal income than corporate income.

9. For the interpretation and possible explanations of this result, see Mulligan *et al.* (2004) and Chapters 2 and 3.

7. Data appendix: list of all variables and their sources

POLITY2: The revised POLITY score is computed by subtracting the AUTOC score from the DEMOC score. The resulting unified polity scale ranges from +10 (strongly democratic) to −10 (strongly autocratic). Source: Polity IV dataset (2007).

DEMOC: The democracy indicator is an additive 11-point scale (0–10). It is derived from coding the competitiveness of political participation, the openness and competitiveness of executive recruitment and constraints on the chief executive (specific variables in the Polity IV dataset) using different weights. The standardized score for more complex transition situations that result in unintended institutional arrangements is −88. Source: Polity IV dataset (2007).

AUTOC: The autocracy indicator is an additive 11-point scale (0–10). It is derived from coding the competitiveness of political participation, the regulation of participation, the openness and competitiveness of executive recruitment and constraints on the chief executive (specific variables in the Polity IV dataset) using different weights. The standardized score for more complex transition situations that result in unintended institutional arrangements is −88. Source: Polity IV dataset (2007).

DURABLE: It measures the regime durability, that is the number of years since the most recent regime change (defined by a three-point change in the POLITY score over a period of three years or less) or the end of a transition period defined by the lack of stable political institutions (denoted by a standardized authority score). In calculating the DURABLE value, the first year during which a new (post-change) polity is established is coded as the baseline 'year zero' (value = 0) and each subsequent year adds one to the value of the DURABLE variable consecutively until a new regime change or transition period occurs. Source: Polity IV dataset (2007).

FREEDOM1: Civil liberties, conceived of as freedoms to develop views, organizations and personal autonomy apart from the state.

They are measured on a 1-to-7 scale, with 1 representing the highest degree of freedom and 7 the lowest. Countries are assigned particular scores based on evaluations in relation to a pre-established checklist of questions related to freedom of expression, freedom of organization, freedom of assembly, property rights protection, equality under the law, etc. Source: Freedom House (various years), *Freedom of the World: The Annual Survey of Political Rights and Civil Liberties*, Washington, DC and New York: Rowman & Littlefield, http://www.freedomhouse.org.

FREEDOM2: Political rights, conceived of as rights that enable people to participate freely in the political process. They are measured on a 1-to-7 scale, with 1 representing the highest degree of freedom and 7 the lowest. Countries are assigned a particular score based on evaluations by a team of regional experts and scholars in relation to a pre-established checklist of questions dealing with the existence of free and fair elections, the right to organize, the existence of a credible opposition, avoidance of corruption, etc. Source: Freedom House (various years), *Freedom of the World: The Annual Survey of Political Rights and Civil Liberties*, Washington, DC and New York: Rowman & Littlefield, http://www.freedomhouse.org.

TAX_REV: Tax revenue/GDP or total fiscal pressure/GDP. For Asian countries *TAX_REV* is tax revenue/GDP, computed by us. Data on tax revenue (in national currency, referred to central government with the exception of Vietnam) come from IMF (1999, 2001–06), *Government Finance Statistics Yearbook*. Data on GDP (in national currency) come from IMF (2008), *World Economic Outlook Database*. For Latin American countries *TAX_REV* is total fiscal pressure/GDP. Source: CEPALSTAT, http://websie. eclac.cl/sisgen/ConsultaIntegrada.asp. For new EU members *TAX_REV* is total fiscal pressure/GDP. Source: Eurostat (2007), *Taxation Trends in the European Union*, Eurostat Statistical Book, and L. Bernardi, M. Chandler and L. Gandullia (eds) (2005), *Tax Systems and Tax Reforms in New EU Members*, London: Routledge.

PIT: Personal income tax/GDP. For Asian countries, computed by us. Data on individual tax on income, profits and capital gains (in national currency, referred to central government with the exception of Vietnam) come from IMF (1999, 2001–06), *Government Finance Statistics Yearbook*. Data on GDP (in national currency) come from IMF (2008), *World Economic Outlook Database*. Not available for

Singapore. For Latin American countries, source: CEPALSTAT, http://websie.eclac.cl/sisgen/ConsultaIntegrada.asp, and L. Bernardi, A. Barreix, A. Marenzi and P. Profeta (eds) (2008), *Tax Systems and Tax Reforms in Latin America*, London: Routledge. Not available for Costa Rica, Ecuador, Nicaragua and Uruguay. For new EU members, source: Eurostat (2007), *Taxation Trends in the European Union*, Eurostat Statistical Book, and L. Bernardi, M. Chandler and L. Gandullia (eds) (2005), *Tax Systems and Tax Reforms in New EU Members*, London: Routledge.

CIT: Corporate income tax/GDP. For Asian countries, computed by us. Data on corporate tax on income, profits and capital gains (in national currency, referred to central government with the exception of Vietnam) come from IMF (1999, 2001–06), *Government Finance Statistics Yearbook*. Data on GDP (in national currency) come from IMF (2008), *World Economic Outlook Database*. Not available for Singapore. For Latin American countries, source: CEPALSTAT, http://websie.eclac.cl/sisgen/ConsultaIntegrada.asp, and L. Bernardi, A. Barreix, A. Marenzi and P. Profeta (eds) (2008), *Tax Systems and Tax Reforms in Latin America*, London: Routledge. Not available for Costa Rica, Ecuador and Nicaragua. For new EU members, source: Eurostat (2007), *Taxation Trends in the European Union*, Eurostat Statistical Book, and L. Bernardi, M. Chandler and L. Gandullia (eds) (2005), *Tax Systems and Tax Reforms in New EU Members*, London: Routledge.

PROP: Taxes on property/GDP. For Asian countries, computed by us. Data on taxes on property (in national currency, referred to central government with the exception of Vietnam) come from IMF (1999, 2001–06), *Government Finance Statistics Yearbook*. Data on GDP (in national currency) come from IMF (2008), *World Economic Outlook Database*. For Latin American countries, source: CEPALSTAT, http://websie.eclac.cl/sisgen/ConsultaIntegrada.asp. For new EU members, not available.

TRADE: Taxes on international trade, transactions/GDP. For Asian countries, computed by us. Data on taxes on international trade, transactions (in national currency, referred to central government with the exception of Vietnam) come from IMF (1999, 2001–06), *Government Finance Statistics Yearbook*. Data on GDP (in national currency) come from IMF (2008), *World Economic Outlook Database*. For Latin American countries, source: CEPALSTAT, http://websie.eclac.cl/sisgen/ConsultaIntegrada.asp. For new EU members *TRADE* is other taxes on products (incl. import duties), source: Eurostat (2007), *Taxation Trends in the European Union*, Eurostat Statistical Book.

GS: Domestic taxes on goods and services/GDP or indirect taxes/ GDP. For Asian countries *GS* is domestic taxes on goods and services/GDP, computed by us. Data on domestic taxes on goods and services (in national currency, referred to central government with the exception of Vietnam) come from IMF (1999, 2001–06), *Government Finance Statistics Yearbook*. Data on GDP (in national currency, at constant market prices) come from IMF (2008), *World Economic Outlook Database*. For Latin American countries *GS* is indirect taxes/GDP. Source: CEPALSTAT, http://websie.eclac.cl/ sisgen/ConsultaIntegrada.asp. For new EU members, *GS* is indirect taxes/GDP. Source: Eurostat (2007), *Taxation Trends in the European Union*, Eurostat Statistical Book, and L. Bernardi, M. Chandler and L. Gandullia (eds) (2005), *Tax Systems and Tax Reforms in New EU Members*, London: Routledge.

SS: Social security contributions/GDP. For Asian countries, computed by us. Data on social security contributions (in national currency, referred to central government with the exception of Vietnam) come from IMF (1999, 2001–06), *Government Finance Statistics Yearbook*. Data on GDP (in national currency) come from IMF (2008), *World Economic Outlook Database*. Not available for China, Pakistan, the Philippines, Singapore and Vietnam. For Latin American countries, source: CEPALSTAT, http://websie.eclac.cl/ sisgen/ConsultaIntegrada.asp. Not available for Haiti. For new EU members, source: Eurostat (2007), *Taxation Trends in the European Union*, Eurostat Statistical Book, and L. Bernardi, M. Chandler and L. Gandullia (eds) (2005), *Tax Systems and Tax Reforms in New EU Members*, London: Routledge.

DIRECT: Direct taxes/GDP or tax on income, profits and capital gains/GDP. For Asian countries *DIRECT* is tax on income, profits and capital gains/GDP, computed by us. Data on tax on income, profits and capital gains (in national currency, referred to central government with the exception of Vietnam) come from IMF (1999, 2001–06), *Government Finance Statistics Yearbook*. Data on GDP (in national currency) come from IMF (2008), *World Economic Outlook Database*. For Latin American countries *DIRECT* is direct taxes (net of property taxes)/GDP. Source: CEPALSTAT, http://websie.eclac. cl/sisgen/ConsultaIntegrada.asp. For new EU members, *DIRECT* is direct taxes/GDP. Source: Eurostat (2007), *Taxation Trends in the European Union*, Eurostat Statistical Book, and L. Bernardi, M. Chandler and L. Gandullia (eds) (2005), *Tax Systems and Tax Reforms in New EU Members*, London: Routledge.

INDIRECT: Indirect taxes/GDP or domestic taxes on goods and services/GDP. For Asian countries *INDIRECT* is domestic taxes on goods and services/GDP, computed by us. Data on domestic taxes on goods and services (in national currency, referred to central government with the exception of Vietnam) come from IMF (1999, 2001–06), *Government Finance Statistics Yearbook*. Data on GDP (in national currency) come from IMF (2008), *World Economic Outlook Database*. For Latin American countries *INDIRECT* is indirect taxes (net of trade taxes)/GDP. Source: CEPALSTAT, http://websie.eclac.cl/sisgen/ConsultaIntegrada.asp. For new EU members *INDIRECT* is indirect taxes (net of trade taxes)/GDP. Source: Eurostat (2007), *Taxation Trends in the European Union*, Eurostat Statistical Book, and L. Bernardi, M. Chandler and L. Gandullia (eds) (2005), *Tax Systems and Tax Reforms in New EU Members*, London: Routledge.

GDPVAR: Growth rate of real GDP per capita (percentage in 2000 constant prices: chain series). Source: A. Heston, R. Summers and B. Aten (2006), *Penn World Table*, Version 6.2, Center for International Comparisons of Production, Income and Prices at the University of Pennsylvania.

LGDP: Log real GDP chain per worker (I$ per worker in 2000 constant prices). Source: A. Heston, R. Summers and B. Aten (2006), *Penn World Table*, Version 6.2, Center for International Comparisons of Production, Income and Prices at the University of Pennsylvania.

OPE: The sum of exports and imports as a percentage of GDP. Source: DataGob, Government Indicators Database, http://www.iadb.org/DataGob/. Data are based on World Bank, *World Development Indicators (WDI) Online*, Washington, DC: World Bank, http://devdata.worldbank.org/dataonline. Not available for Singapore.

DEBT: Central government debt/GDP for Asian and Latin American countries. Source: U. Panizza (2006), *Public Debt around the World: A New Dataset of Central Government Debt*, IADB, http://www.iadb.org/res/pub_desc.cfm?pub_id=DBA-005.   Not available for Vietnam and the Dominican Republic. General gov-

ernment debt/GDP for new EU members. Source: Eurostat, http://
epp.eurostat.ec.europa.eu/portal/page?_pageid=1090,30070682,109
0_33076576&_dad=portal&_schema=PORTAL and OECD (2008),
Factbook: Economic, Environmental and Social Statistics.

AGR: The share of agriculture as a percentage of GDP. For Asian
countries, source: Asian Development Bank (various years), *Key
Indicators*. For Latin American countries, computed by us from
CEPALSTAT data, http://websie.eclac.cl/sisgen/ConsultaIntegrada.
asp. Not available for Guatemala. For new EU members, not
available.

OLD: Population ages 65 and above as percentage of total.
Source: World Bank (2007), *World Development Indicators (WDI
2007)*, Washington, DC: World Bank.

FEMALE: Female labour force participation rate as percentage
of female population ages 15–64. Source: World Bank (2007), *World
Development Indicators (WDI 2007)*, Washington, DC: World
Bank.

URBAN: Percentage of urban population over the total population. Source: World Bank (2007), *World Development Indicators
(WDI 2007)*, Washington, DC: World Bank.

DENSITY: Number of people per square kilometre Source:
World Bank (2007), *World Development Indicators (WDI 2007)*,
Washington, DC: World Bank.

SCHOOLING: School enrolment, secondary (percentage net).
For Latin American countries *SCHOOLING* is school enrolment,
secondary (percentage gross). Source: World Bank (2007), *World
Development Indicators (WDI 2007)*, Washington, DC: World Bank.
Not available for China, India, Singapore, Sri Lanka, Thailand,
Haiti, Uruguay, the Czech Republic, Latvia and Slovakia.

SHADOW: The share of shadow economy as a percentage of
GDP. Source: (i) F. Schneider (2005), 'Shadow Economies around
the World: What Do We Really Know?', *European Journal of
Political Economy*, 21, 598–642; (ii) F. Schneider (2007), 'Shadow
Economies and Corruption All Over the World: New Estimates
for 145 Countries', *Economics: The Open Access, Open Assessment
E-Journal*, 2007-9. Not available for Cyprus.

GINI: Gini index on a zero-to-100 scale. Source: World Bank
(2007), *World Development Indicators (WDI 2007)*, Washington,
DC: World Bank. Not available for South Korea and Cyprus.

CREDIT: Private credit by deposit money bank/GDP. Source:

World Bank (2007), *World Development Indicators (WDI 2007)*, Washington, DC: World Bank. Not available for Vietnam.

CREDIT2: Private credit by deposit money bank and other financial instruments/GDP. Source: World Bank (2007), *World Development Indicators (WDI 2007)*, Washington, DC: World Bank. Not available for Vietnam.

Bibliography

Acemoglu, D. and J.A. Robinson (2006), *Economic Origins of Dictatorship and Democracy*, New York: Cambridge University Press.

Acemoglu, D., S. Johnson, J.A. Robinson and P. Yared (2004), 'From Education to Democracy', Mimeo, MIT.

Acemoglu, D., S. Johnson, J.A. Robinson and P. Yared (2005), 'Income and Democracy', Mimeo, MIT.

Afonso, J.R. (2001), *Brazil: Fiscal Federalism, Tax Modernization and Consumption and Production Taxes*, São Paulo: SF/BNDES.

Aghion, P., E. Caroli and C. García–Peñalosa (1999), 'Inequality and Economic Growth: The Perspective of the New Growth Theories', *Journal of Economic Literature*, 37 (4), 1615–60.

Ahmad, S.E. and N.H. Stern (1991), *The Theory and Practice of Tax Reform in Developing Countries*, Cambridge: Cambridge University Press.

Alesina, A. and R. Perotti (1996), 'Income Distribution, Political Instability, and Investment', *European Economic Review*, 78, 796–805.

Allingham, M.G. and A. Sandmo (1972), 'Income Tax Evasion: A Theoretical Analysis', *Journal of Public Economics*, 1, 323–38.

Alm, J. (1996), 'Explaining Tax Compliance', in S. Pozo (ed.), *Exploring the Underground Economy: Studies of Illegal and Unreported Activity*, Kalamazoo, MI: W.E. Upjohn Institute for Employment Research.

Ansari, M. (1982), 'Determinants of Tax Ratio: A Cross-Country Analysis', *Economic and Political Weekly*, June 19, pp. 1035–1042.

Barreix, A., J. Roca and L. Villela (2006), *La Equidad Fiscal en Los Paises Andinos*, Washington, DC: DFID, BID, CAN.

Barro, R.J. (1979), 'On the Determination of the Public Debt', *Journal of Political Economy*, 87, 940–71.

Barro, R.J. (1996), 'Democracy and Growth', *Journal of Economic Growth*, 1, 1–27.

Barro, R.J. (1999), 'The Determinants of Democracy', *Journal of Political Economy*, 107, S158–S183.

Bates, R.H. (1991), 'The Economics of Transition to Democracy', *PS: Political Science and Politics*, 24, 24–7.

Bates, R.H. and Da-Hsiang D. Lien (1985), 'A Note on Taxation, Development and Representative Government', *Politics and Society*, 14, 53–70.

Becker, G.S. (1983), 'A Theory of Competition among Pressure Groups for Political Influence', *Quarterly Journal of Economics*, 98, 371–400.

Bernardi, L. and P. Profeta (eds) (2004), *Tax Systems and Tax Reforms in Europe*, London: Routledge.

Bernardi, L., M. Chandler and L. Gandullia (eds) (2005), *Tax Systems and Tax Reforms in New EU Members*, London: Routledge.

Bernardi, L., A. Fraschini and P. Shome (eds) (2006), *Tax Systems and Tax Reforms in South and East Asia*, London: Routledge.

Bernardi, L., A. Barreix, A. Marenzi and P. Profeta (eds) (2008), *Tax Systems and Tax Reforms in Latin America*, London: Routledge.

Bird, R.M. (1974), *Taxing Agricultural Land in Developing Countries*, Cambridge: Harvard University Press.

Boix, C. (2003), *Democracy and Redistribution*, New York: Cambridge University Press.

Bollen, K.A. and R.W. Jackman (1985), 'Political Democracy and the Size Distribution of Income', *American Sociological Review*, 60, 438–57.

Burgess, R. and N. Stern (1993), 'Taxation and Development', *Journal of Economic Literature*, 31, 762–830.

Chelliah, R.J. (1971), 'Trends in Taxation in Developing Countries', *IMF Staff Papers*, 18, 254–331.

CIA (2008), *The World Factbook*, https://www.cia.gov/library/publications/the-world-factbook/index.html.

Collier, R.B. (1999), *Paths towards Democracy: The Working Class and Elites in Western Europe and South America*, New York: Cambridge University Press.

Colomer, J.M. (2000), *Strategic Transitions: Game Theory and Democratization*, Baltimore, MD: Johns Hopkins University Press.

Dahl, R.A. (1971), *Polyarchy: Participation and Opposition*, New Haven, CT: Yale University Press.

de Juan, A., M. Lasheres and R. Mayo (1994), 'Voluntary Tax

Compliant Behavior of Spanish Income Tax Payers', *Public Finance*, 49, 90–105.

Diamond, L. (1996) 'Is the Third Wave Over?', *Journal of Democracy*, 7, 20–37.

Di Nardo, J.E., N. M. Fortin and T. Lemieux (1996), 'Labour Market Institutions and the Distribution of Wages, 1973–1992: A Semiparametric Approach', *Econometrica*, 65, 1001–44.

Di Palma, G. (1990), *To Craft Democracies*, Berkeley: University of California Press.

Djankov, S., R. La Porta, F. Lopez-de-Silanes and A. Shleifer (2003), 'The New Comparative Economics', *Journal of Comparative Economics*, 31 (4), 595–619.

Drake, P.W. (1996), *Labor Movements and Dictatorships: The Southern Cone in Comparative Perspective*, Baltimore, MD: Johns Hopkins University Press.

EBRD (1999), *Transition Report*, London: European Bank for Reconstruction and Development.

Ebrill, L., M. Keen, J.P. Bodin and V. Summers (2001), *The Modern VAT*, Washington, DC: International Monetary Fund.

Epstein, D.L., R. Bates, J. Goldstone, I. Kristensen and S. O'Halloran (2005), 'Democratic Transitions', CID Working Paper no. 101, Harvard University, J.F.K. School of Government.

Feld, L.P. and B.S. Frey (2002), 'Trust Breeds Trust: How Taxpayers Are Treated', *Economics of Governance*, 3, 87–99.

Fernandez, R. and D. Rodrik (1991), 'Resistance to Reform: Status Quo Bias in the Presence of Individual-Specific Uncertainty', *American Economic Review*, 81 (5), 1146–55.

Fidrmuc, J. (2003), 'Economic Reform, Democracy, and Growth during Post-Communist Transition', *European Journal of Political Economy*, 19 (2), 583–604.

Galasso, V., R. Gatti and P. Profeta (2009), 'Investing for the Old Age: Pensions, Children and Savings', *International Tax and Public Finance*, 16 (4), 538–59.

Gerring, J., P. Bond, W.T. Barndt and C. Moreno (2005), 'Democracy and Economic Growth: A Historical Perspective', *World Politics*, 57 (1), 323–64.

Ghura, D. (1998), 'Tax Revenue in Sub-Saharan Africa: Effects of Economic Policies and Corruption', IMF Working Paper 98/135, International Monetary Fund, Washington, DC.

Giavazzi, F. and G. Tabellini (2005), 'Economic and Political

Liberalizations', *Journal of Monetary Economics*, 52 (7), 1297–1330.

Giles, D.E.A. and L.M. Tedds (2002), 'Taxes and the Canadian Underground Economy', Canadian Tax Paper no. 106, Canadian Tax Foundation, Toronto.

Glaeser, E., R. La Porta, F. Lopez-de-Silanes and A. Shleifer (2004), 'Do Institutions Cause Growth?', *Journal of Economic Growth*, 9, 271–303.

Gómez Sabaini, J.C. and R. Martner (2008), 'Taxation Structure and Main Tax Policy Issues', in L. Bernardi, A. Barreix, A. Marenzi and P. Profeta (eds), *Tax Systems and Tax Reforms in Latin America*, London: Routledge.

Goode, R. (1972), 'Personal Income Taxation in Latin America', in Joint Tax Program, OAS/IDB/ECLA, *Fiscal Policy for Economic Growth in Latin America*, Baltimore, MD: Johns Hopkins University Press.

Gordon, R. and W. Li (2005a) 'Tax Structure in Developing Countries: Many Puzzles and a Possible Explanation', NBER Working Paper 11267.

Gordon, R. and W. Li (2005b) 'Puzzling Tax Structures in Developing Countries: A Comparison of Two Alternative Explanations', NBER Working Paper 11661.

Grossman, G.M. and E. Helpman (1994), 'Protection for Sale', *American Economic Review*, 84 (4), 833–50.

Gupta, A.S. (2007), 'Determinants of Tax Revenue Efforts in Developing Countries', IMF Working Papers 07/184, International Monetary Fund.

Haggard, S. and R.R. Kaufman (1995), *The Political Economy of Democratic Transitions*, Princeton, NJ: Princeton University Press.

Hayek, F.A. (1960), *The Constitution of Liberty*, Chicago: University of Chicago Press.

Hettich, W. and S.L. Winer (1999), *Democratic Choice and Taxation: A Theoretical and Empirical Analysis*, New York: Cambridge University Press.

Higley, J. and R. Gunther (eds) (1992), *Elites and Democratic Consolidation in Latin America and Southern Europe*, New York: Cambridge University Press.

Hinrichs, H.H. (1966), *A General Theory of Tax Structure: Change during Economic Development*, Cambridge, MA: Harvard Law School International Tax Program.

Huber, E. and J. Stephens (1999), 'The Bourgeoisie and Democracy: Historical and Comparative Perspectives', *Social Research*, 66, 759–88.

Huntington, S.P. (1968), *Political Order in Changing Societies*, New Haven, CT: Yale University Press.

Huntington, S.P. (1991), *The Third Wave: Democratization in the Late Twentieth Century*, Norman: University of Oklahoma Press.

IBFD (2006), Latin America – Taxation and Investment, CD ROM 1/2006, Amsterdam: International Bureau of Fiscal Documentation.

Jacobs, D. (1998), 'Social Welfare Systems in East Asia: A Comparative Analysis Including Private Welfare,' Case paper 10, Centre for Analysis of Social Exclusion, Sticerd LSE.

Johnson, S., D. Kaufmann and P. Zoido-Lobatón (1998a), 'Regulatory Discretion and the Unofficial Economy', *American Economic Review*, 88 (2), 387–92.

Johnson, S., D. Kaufmann and P. Zoido-Lobatón (1998b), 'Corruption, Public Finances and the Unofficial Economy', World Bank Discussion Paper, World Bank, Washington, DC.

Kaufman, R.R. and B. Stallings (1991), 'The Political Economy of Latin American Populism', in R. Dornbusch and S. Edwards (eds), *The Macroeconomics of Populism in Latin America*, Chicago: University of Chicago Press.

Keen, M. and A. Simone (2004), 'Tax Policy in Developing Countries: Some Lessons from the 1990s and Some Challenges Ahead', in S. Gupta, B. Clements and G. Inchauste (eds), *Helping Countries Develop: The Role of Fiscal Policy*, Washington, DC: International Monetary Fund.

Kenny, L.W. and S.L. Winer (2006), 'Tax Systems in the World: An Empirical Investigation into the Importance of Tax Bases, Administration Costs, Scale and Political Regime', *International Tax and Public Finance*, 13 (2/3), 181–215.

Lichbach, M.I. (1989), 'An Evaluation of "Does Economic Inequality Breed Political Conflict?" Studies', *World Politics*, 41, 431–70.

Lijphart, A. (1990), 'The Southern European Examples of Democratization: Six Lessons for Latin America', *Government and Opposition*, 25 (1), 68–84.

Linz, J.J. (1978), *Crisis, Breakdown and Re-equilibration*, Baltimore, MD: Johns Hopkins University Press.

Linz, J.J. and A. Stepan (1978), *The Breakdown of Democratic Regimes*, Baltimore, MD: Johns Hopkins University Press.

Linz, J.J. and A. Stepan (1996), *Problems of Democratic Transition and Consolidation: Southern Europe, South America, and Post-Communist Europe*, Baltimore, MD: Johns Hopkins University Press.

Lippert, O. and M. Walker (eds) (1997), *The Underground Economy: Global Evidences of its Size and Impact*, Vancouver, BC: Frazer Institute.

Lipset, S.M. (1959), 'Some Social Prerequisites for Democracy: Economic Development and Political Legitimacy', *American Political Science Review*, 53, 69–105.

Luebbert, G. (1991), *Liberalism, Fascism or Social Democracy: Social Classes and the Political Origins of Regimes in Interwar Europe*, New York: Oxford University Press.

Luna, J.P. and E.J. Zechmeister (2005), 'Political Representation in Latin America', *Comparative Political Studies*, 38 (4), 388–416.

Maffini, G. and A. Marenzi (2008), 'Corporate Tax Systems and Policies for Attracting FDI', in L. Bernardi, A. Barreix, A. Marenzi and P. Profeta (eds), *Tax Systems and Tax Reforms in Latin America*, London: Routledge.

Meltzer, A.H. and S.F. Richard (1981), 'A Rational Theory of the Size of Government', *Journal of Political Economy*, 89, 914–27.

Mitra, P. and N. Stern (2003), 'Tax Systems in Transition', World Bank Policy Research Working Paper 2947.

Moore, B. (1966), *The Social Origins of Dictatorship and Democracy: Lord and Peasant in the Making of the Modern World*, Boston, MA: Beacon Press.

Muller, E.N. (1995), 'Economic Determinants of Democracy', *American Sociological Review*, 60, 966–82.

Mulligan, C.B., R. Gil and X. Sala-i-Martin (2004), 'Do Democracies Have Different Public Policies than Non Democracies?', *Journal of Economic Perspectives*, 18 (1), 51–74.

Musgrave, R.A. (1969), *Fiscal Systems*, New Haven, CT: Yale University Press.

O'Donnell, G. (1973), *Modernization and Bureaucratic Authoritarianism: Studies in South American Politics*, Berkeley: University of California, Institute for International Studies.

O'Donnell, G. (1988), 'Challenges to Democratization in Brazil', *World Policy Journal*, 5, 281–300.

O'Donnell, G. and P.C. Schmitter (1986), *Transitions from*

Authoritarian Rule: Tentative Conclusions about Uncertain Democracies, Baltimore. MD: Johns Hopkins University Press.

OECD (1991), *The Role of Tax Reform in Central and Eastern European Economies*, Paris: OECD.

OECD (2008), *OECD Factbook 2008: Economic, Environmental and Social Statistics*, Paris: OECD.

Papaioannou, E. and G. Siourounis (2008), 'Democratization and Growth', *Economic Journal*, 118, 1520–51.

Peltzman, S. (1980), 'The Growth of Government', *Journal of Law and Economics*, 23, 209–87.

Persson, T. (2005), 'Forms of Democracy, Policy and Economic Development', CEPR Discussion Paper 4938.

Persson, T. and G. Tabellini (2007), 'The Growth Effect of Democracy: Is It Heterogeneous and How Can It Be Estimated?', NBER Working Paper 13150.

Pommerehne, W. and H. Weck-Hannemann (1996), 'Tax Rates, Tax Administration and Income Tax Evasion in Switzerland', *Public Choice*, 88, 161–70.

Profeta, P. (2007), 'Political Support and Tax Reforms with an Application to Italy', *Public Choice*, 131 (1–2), 141–55.

Profeta, P. and S. Scabrosetti (2008), 'Political Economy Issues of Taxation', in L. Bernardi, A. Barreix, A. Marenzi and P. Profeta (eds), *Tax Systems and Tax Reforms in Latin America*, London: Routledge.

Profeta, P., M. Cacciatore and S. Scabrosetti (2006), 'Democracy and Welfare without Welfare State', in L. Bernardi, A. Fraschini and P. Shome (eds), *Tax Systems and Tax Reforms in South and East Asia*, London: Routledge.

Przeworski, A., M. Alvarez, J.A. Cheibub and F. Limonigi (2000), *Democracy and Development: Political Institutions and Material Well-Being in the World: 1950–1990*, New York: Cambridge University Press.

Rodriguez, F. (2001), 'The Political Economy of Latin American Economic Growth', Global Development Network Research Paper.

Rodrik, D. (1998), 'Why Do More Open Economies have Bigger Governments?', *Journal of Political Economy*, 106, 997–1032.

Rodrik, D. and R. Wacziarg (2005), 'Do Democratic Transitions Produce Bad Economic Outcomes?', *American Economic Review Papers and Proceedings*, 95 (2), 50–55.

Rogowski, R. (1998), 'Democracy, Capital, Skill, and Country Size: Effects of Asset Mobility and Regime Monopoly on the Odds of Democratic Rule', in P.W. Drake, and M.D. McCubbins (eds), *The Origins of Liberty*, Princeton, NJ: Princeton University Press.

Roland, G. (2001), 'Ten Years After . . . Transition and Economics', *IMF Staff Papers*, 48, Special Issue, 29–52.

Roland, G. (2002), 'The Political Economy of Transition', *Journal of Economic Perspectives*, 16, 29–50.

Rueschemeyer, D., E.H. Stephens and J.D. Stephens (1992), *Capitalist Development and Democracy*, Chicago: University of Chicago Press.

Santiso, J. (2006), *Latin America's Political Economy of the Possible*, Cambridge, MA: MIT Press.

Schaffer, M. and G. Turley (2000), 'Effective versus Statutory Taxation: Measuring Effective Tax Administration in Transition Economies', Working Paper 347, William Davidson Institute at University of Michigan.

Schneider, F. (1994), 'Can the Shadow Economy Be Reduced through Major Tax Reforms? An Empirical Investigation for Austria', *Supplement to Public Finance/Finances Publiques*, 49, 137–52.

Schneider, F. (2000), 'The Increase of the Size of the Shadow Economy of 18 OECD Countries: Some Preliminary Explanations', Paper presented at the Annual Public Choice Meeting, March, Charleston, SC.

Schneider, F. (2005), 'Shadow Economies around the World: What Do We Really Know?', *European Journal of Political Economy*, 21, 598–642.

Schneider, F. (2007), 'Shadow Economies and Corruption All Over the World: New Estimates for 145 Countries', *Economics: The Open Access, Open Assessment E-Journal*, 2007–9.

Schneider, F. and D. Enste (2000), 'Shadow Economies: Size, Causes, and Consequences', *Journal of Economic Literature*, 38 (1), 77–114.

Schumpeter, J.A. (1942), *Capitalism, Socialism and Democracy*, New York: Harper & Brothers.

Shin, D.C. (1994), 'On the Third Wave of Democratization: A Synthesis and Evaluation of Recent Theory and Research', *World Politics*, 47, 135–70.

Stepan, A. (1985), 'State Power and the Strength of Civil Society in the Southern Cone of Latin America', in P.B. Evans, D. Rueschemeyer and T. Skocpol (eds), *Bringing the State Back In*, New York: Cambridge University Press.

Stigler, G.J. (1970), 'Director's Law of Public Income Redistribution', *Journal of Law and Economics*, 13, 1–10.

Stotsky, J.G. and A. WoldeMariam (1997), 'Tax Effort in Sub-Saharan Africa', IMF Working Paper 97/107, International Monetary Fund, Washington, DC.

Tanzi, V. (1966), 'Personal Income Taxation in Latin America: Obstacles and Possibilities', *National Tax Journal*, XIX, 2.

Tanzi, V. (1987), 'Quantitative Characteristics of the Tax Systems of Developing Countries', in D.M.G. Newbery and N.H. Stern (eds), *The Theory of Taxation for Developing Countries*, New York: Oxford University Press.

Tanzi, V. (1992), 'Structural Factors and Tax Revenue in Developing Countries: A Decade of Evidence', in I. Goldin and L.A. Winters (eds), *Open Economies: Structural Adjustment and Agriculture*, New York: Cambridge University Press.

Tanzi, V. (1999), 'Uses and Abuses of Estimates of the Underground Economy', *Economic Journal*, 109 (456), 338–40.

Tanzi, V. (2005), 'Foreword: Tax Systems and Tax Reforms in Transition Economies', in L. Bernardi, M. Chandler and L. Gandullia (eds), *Tax Systems and Tax Reforms in New EU Members*, London: Routledge.

Tanzi, V. (2008), 'Introduction: Tax Systems and Tax Reforms in Latin America', in L. Bernardi, A. Barreix, A. Marenzi and P. Profeta (eds), *Tax Systems and Tax Reforms in Latin America*, London: Routledge.

Tanzi, V. and L. Schuknecht (1997), 'Reconsidering the Fiscal Role of Government: The International Perspective', *American Economic Review*, 87 (2), 164–8.

Tanzi, V. and G. Tsibouris (2000), 'Fiscal Reform over Ten Years of Transition', IMF Working Paper 00/113, International Monetary Fund, Washington, DC.

Therborn, G. (1977), 'The Rule of Capital and the Rise of Democracy', *New Left Review*, 103, 3–41.

Thomas, J.J. (1992), *Informal Economic Activity*, LSE Handbooks in Economics, London: Harvester Wheatsheaf.

Tilly, C. (2004), *Contention and Democracy in Europe, 1650–2000*, New York: Cambridge University Press.

Tullock, G. (1987), *Autocracy*, Boston, MA: Kluwer Academic Publishers.

Wintrobe, R. (1990), 'The Tinpot and the Totalitarian: An Economic Theory of Dictatorship', *American Political Science Review*, 84, 849–72.

Wittman, D. (1989), 'Why Democracies Produce Efficient Results', *Journal of Political Economy*, 97, 1395–424.

World Bank (1999), *Towards an East Asian Social Protection Strategy*, Washington: World Bank.

Index

new EU member countries 26–7,
134–5
tax design and composition
39–41, 42, 43, 44, 45, 46
and tax revenue 31, 32
population density 171
Asia 69–70, 71
comparative analysis 149, 154–5,
158
Latin America 104–19
and tax revenue 36, 38
Préval, R. 130
private credit 72, 172
property taxes 16–17, 45, 168
Asia 54, 75, 80–81, 82
Latin America 97–100, 102, 119,
121
new EU member countries 145
proportional representation 10, 12
Przeworski, A. 12, 24, 29
public insurance 15–16
public sector 14–16
public spending 15–16, 31, 141
public support for democracy 94

quality of democracy 120–21, 121–4

redistribution 3, 6, 7, 31, 47, 89, 164
democracy and 14–17
Reina, C.R. 130
rent-seeking 140
representation 120–21, 122–3
repression 5, 16
Revolutionary Armed Forces of
Colombia (FARC) 128
Robinson, J.A. 5, 9, 14
Rodríguez, A. 132
Rodríguez, E. 127
Rodriguez, F. 89
Rodrik, D. 12, 13–14, 23
Roland, G. 137, 139
Ruiz-Tagle, F. 128

Sánchez de Lozada, G. 127
Sandinista National Liberation
Front (FSLN) 131
Sandmo, A. 37

Sanguinetti, J.M. 133
Santiso, J. 94
Schaffer, M. 139
Schneider, F. 37, 38
schooling *see* education
Schuknecht, L. 38
Schumpeter, J.A. 24
seigniorage 17
shadow economy 145, 171
Asia 72, 73–4
comparative analysis 149, 156–7,
158
Latin America 101, 104, 117–18
and tax revenue 36–9
Sharif, N. 84
Shin, D.C. 6, 9
Shinawatra, T. 87
Shining Path 132
shocks, economic 6, 10
Simone, A. 23
Singapore 50, 53, 54–5, 57, 86
Siourounis, G. 11
Slovakia 134, 142, 143–4
Slovenia 134, 142, 143–4
small firms 145
social conflict 7, 123
social mobility 7
social networks 140
social protection 50
social security contributions 39, 47,
169
Asia 54–5, 56, 78–9, 82
comparative analysis 162–3, 164
Latin America 97–100, 101,
102–3, 119, 121
new EU member countries 142,
143, 144
and political variables 45, 46
sociodemographic variables 3
Asia 58–9, 60–72, 73–4
comparative analysis 149, 150–59
Latin America 104–19
and tax revenue 31–9
socio-economic conditions
Asia 49–50
determinants of democracy 5–11
Sri Lanka 50, 53, 54–5, 57, 86